MW01612252

Kim Gentes watches the world with a thoughtful eye . . . he sees things that others miss. In the world of worship resources he has married creativity, diligence and ingenuity, and he has done this for many years. All of his work related to worship materials and practices grows out of his excellent character and true passion for Christ and His Church.

Dr. Peter Fitch, Dean of Ministry Studies, St. Stephen's University

My friend, Kim Gentes, has put together a guide that should be on the desk of every worship leader or music minister. It is helpful, clear, unbiased and saves churches time and money. Kim has spent much of his life dedicated to resourcing the church in worship and this volume is full of that wisdom, made practical for each of us.

Don Moen, Worship Leader, Songwriter, Producer- Nashville, TN

"As a worship resourcer and leader of 20+ years, I have been waiting for the Ultimate Worship Resource Guide. More than the guide itself, I've been waiting for someone like Kim Gentes to put it together. He is an on-the-ground worship leader, ran one of the largest internet worship resourcing stores in the world (WorshipMusic.com), develops tools that simply work for worship leaders (WorshipTeam.com) and is probably the world's most esteemed industry expert when it comes to reviewing worship resources. This Guide is fair, honest, and laced with the kind of practical insight only a fellow worship ministry leader could have. Kim's broad knowledge of the resources available, excellent research, and careful evaluation make this guide indispensable. I will be among the first to own a copy. Every worship leader on the planet should email Kim with a big "thanks" for creating this objective, excellent tool. I'll be the first to say it: Thank you Kim. You have made my work so much easier."

Dan Wilt, M.Min., Founder, WorshipTraining.com

2011 Ultimate Worship Resource Guide: Songs & Media Edition

2011 Ultimate Worship Resource Guide: Songs & Media Edition

The ultimate, edited guide of where to access and purchase church worship resources for leaders, ministers, planners, media techs and musicians.

Kim Anthony Gentes

2011 Ultimate Worship Resource Guide – Songs & Media Edition : The ultimate, edited guide of where to access and purchase church worship resources for leaders, ministers, planners, media techs and musicians.

By Kim Anthony Gentes

Research: Martin Caffrey
Interior Illustration & Artist Photo: Matt Frise (www.mattfrise.com)
Editor: Dan Wilt

©Copyright 2011 Kim Anthony Gentes

ISBN-10: 1460944909
ISBN-13: 978-1460944905

KimGentes.com
6029 Stags Leap Way
Franklin, TN 37064
USA

Contact: wrg@kimgentes.com
More at: www.UltimateWorshipResourceGuide.com

Printed in the United States of America

For my friends in ministry everywhere:
worship leaders, musicians, planners, pastors,
ministers, media techs and visual artists

Contents

To Church Worship Ministry Leaders... 19

Why A Worship Resource Guide?... 21

How To Use This Guide 25

    First Time Readers of The Guide 25

    Experienced Readers of The Guide... 25

    Researching Songs 26

        New Song Discovery 26

        Song Acquisition & Access.. 27

    Researching Media.. 28

The Development of Modern Worship Music Resources: Impacts of History, Style, Promotion & Technology 29

    History 33

        Early Roots and the Jesus People: 60s & 70s....................................... 34

        Expanding Through the Church: The 80s... 35

        Modernization of Style: The 90s... 36

        Popularity And Airplay: 2000 & beyond.. 37

    Changing Name And Style... 39

        Traditional to Popular 39

        The Worship Service's Changing M.O... 40

    More Changes Facilitated by Technology 43

Changes in Promotional Channels for Songs 47

   The Hymnal As The Song Source 47

   Word Of Mouth 47

   Early Continuity Clubs And Events 48

   Radio Writes the Playlist 49

   Music Industry Struggles 49

   Radio Continues 50

Goodbye Hymnal, Hello Chaos: Decades of Change Impact Worship and Music Resources 51

   How The Hymnal Was Replaced 51

   Hymnal to Digital: Timeline Of Worship Resources 53

The Resource Reviews 57

The Rating System 59

Five Star Editor's Choice Resources 61

Church Worship Song Resource Guide 63

   Where To Find New Songs: Search and Discover 63

   WorshipTogether.com 64

   IntegritySongs.com 65

   WorshipTeam.com 66

   CCLI TV 67

   SongQuery.com 68

Digital Worship News 68

SongDiscovery 69

Kim Gentes Reviews 69

Where To Acquire Songs: Online Access And Purchase 71

WorshipTeam.com 72

PraiseCharts.com 73

HymnCharts 74

LifewayWorship.com 75

DiscoverWorship.com 76

WordMusicNow.com 77

GreatWorshipSongs.com 77

Vineyard Resources / Music 78

ION Worship 79

Kingsway Shop 79

J.W.Pepper 80

Cyber Hymnal 81

Hymnal.net 81

CCLI SongSelect 82

MusicNotes.com 83

SheetMusicPlus.com 83

WorshipMusic.com / CBDTunes 84

Software/Digital Files Song Sources 85

X.0: The Digital Hymnal for the Modern Worship Generation (DVD-ROM/Book/CD) 86

The Praise and Worship Song Book (CD-ROM Edition) 87

iWorship Digital Sheet Music Library A-N 88

Worship Together Platinum Series 89

The Paul Baloche Digital Sheet Music Library CD-ROM Songbook 89

Christian Virtual Hymnal 90

SOFTPraise Deluxe 3 Worship Software 91

Continuity Clubs – Contemporary Song Sources 93

SongDiscovery 94

Club Vineyard 95

Spin360 96

Mark Condon iClub 97

Continuity Clubs – Choral Song Sources 99

Brentwood Choral Club 100

Lillenas Choral Club 101

Word Music Choral Club 102

Lifeway Worship Choral Club 103

Praise Gathering Choral Plan 104

Printed/Physical Product Song Sources 105

The Source (Volumes 1, 2, & 3).. 106

Best Of The Best In Contemporary Praise & Worship................... 107

More Songs for Praise & Worship 108

Celebration Hymnal.. 109

Vineyard Music Classics: Top 101 Worship Songs Of The Vineyard Songbook 109

Break Forth Songbook.. 110

The Essential Modern Worship Fakebook.. 111

Worship Together Songbooks – Edition 1.0 through Edition 9.0. 112

Survivor Songbooks... 113

America's 200 Favorite Praise Choruses & Hymns Songbook....... 114

Sing For Joy 115

Wedding & Love Fake Book... 116

Hal Leonard Songbooks 116

Music Instructional Resources For Song Learning.............................. 117

Vertical Music Worship Tools 118

Worship Band Play-Along... 119

Musicademy Song Learner Series 120

New Song Café... 120

Vineyard Toolbox 121

Keyboards – The Songs of Today.. 121

The Essential Worship Band 122

Worship Team Director Vol 1 & 2 122

Video and Image Media Sources 123

Online Media/Image Sites 123

Worship House Media 124

The Work Of The People 125

WorshipVue.com 126

Sermon Spice 127

Willow Arts – Toward Wonder/Pro Video 128

New Worship Media 129

Bluefish TV 130

Forty One Twenty / Church Media 130

iStockphoto 131

Corbis Images 132

Centerline New Media 133

Beamer Films 133

Dan Stevers 134

Digital Stache 135

Thr-Ve 136

Pixelgirl Media 137

WorshipFilms.com 137

A Visual Planet 138

Shift Worship 138

Kinetic Faith 139

Motion Worship 139

Visual Worship 140

Sharefaith 140

Free Media Options 141

Physical Media/Image Sources 143

Midnight Oil 144

Highway Media 144

Nooma Films 145

Digital HotCakes 145

ImageVine 146

Good Salt 146

Song-Based Media/Image Products 147

Worship Backing Band For Churches and Small Groups 148

iWorship DVDs 148

iWorship MPEG Video Library 149

iWorship Flexx 149

Visual Trax DVDs 150

Worship Together Visual – Here I Am To Worship 150

Appendix: Ultimate Worship Resource Guide – Online Tools 153

Acknowledgements 155

About the Author 157

Index 159

For more than 20 years, I have been leading worship, planning services, and training others to do the same. I love serving the church, and am honored to be one of thousands of people who help facilitate the worship and praise life of local churches around the world. Like you, one of the biggest challenges I face is finding quality resources to help my ministry teams as we attempt to administer the worship life of a local church. For the last 13 years, I have spent my vocational life working to resource the worldwide church in worship. For all of that time, I have researched, reviewed, and recommended the best resources I could find for churches.

Some time ago a friend of mine (Arlen Salte) asked me to prepare some resources for a class that he wanted me to teach at his large Break Forth worship conference in Canada. That class would end up being called "Songs and Media Research." Churches around the world were longing for a quality resource guide to help them sift through the thousands of products and services available. I compiled an outline and a general set of notes I felt would be helpful. The next step was to develop a real life compilation of resources in a nicely edited guide. With the help of my good friend Martin Caffrey, who did excellent research for this project, we compiled an initial pass of resources that became the foundation of what you see in this guide. I added to the list extensively, editing and shaping the list to serve the need. I also leaned on some friends who gave expert advice in specific areas. Hearty thanks go to Jeremy Dunn (product resources), Nate Ragan (media) and Dave Williamson (choir) for their helpful thoughts.

Then, I put on my editor's hat and revisited each of the sites as a practical user, investigating, reviewing and editing listings once more. The result is an actual edited guide to great resources and providers of church songs and media. Finally, I wanted to add some contextual information regarding the history of modern worship music resources and the tremendous transition our churches have been going through over the last forty years.

We hope you find this helpful to your ministry.

Serving with you,
Kim Anthony Gentes

Why Do we need a Worship Resource Guide? Good question. Let me answer that for you. In the last 20 years, the proliferation of online data, search and ecommerce options have turned shopping into an experience that happens more and more at your desktop instead of at a mall or brick-and-mortar store. This has helped countless people find resources, evaluate products and shop for better prices. However, what this online world has not done is give us a clear indication of quality, or even allow us to filter through the hundreds of choices available. In fact, now we have so much information at our fingertips that filtering through it has become a full time job. The reason for building the Ultimate Church Worship Resource Guide is to give you *an edited professional church resource guide* that filters out the marketing and notes the top quality companies, products and services we believe should be listed. For a more complete history of how church worship resources have developed over the last thirty years, and why this guide was developed, see the *"The Development of Modern Worship Music Resources: Impacts of History, Style, Promotion & Technology"* on page 29.

What The *Ultimate Church Worship Resource Guide* is my answer to finding resources that are actually helpful, actually effective and ultimately worth spending actual money on. It is an edited list of the finest resources we believe are available today. It is not primarily an advertising listing, unlike many other publications. We all know what happens when you get a publication with every second page filled with advertisements – the publication feels worthless. Every single resource listed in this guide is added and edited by our staff, and reviewed and approved by myself, Kim Gentes. Every company, service or product that appears in these pages is a high quality resource, and has made it in here based on its merit as a resource. We are not paid for inclusion of listings. This is a publication based on our evaluation of quality and impact to local churches, not on marketing campaigns or advertising promotions.

Who

Most church worship services include music and media. This resource is for church leaders, ministers, musicians, media techs, planners and administrators who make worship happen in local churches each and every Sunday. You already have tireless jobs. And while there are thousands of music and media sources for church worship ministries, you just do not have time to filter through them all. Our staff has spent years in church worship resources. This is our job – to resource the church. We have done the work of developing this guide to help you do your job of leading your church in worship.

How

This guide is formatted for function. Sections are meant to help you find what you are looking for quickly. We will review several of these sources in this guide, and give you appropriate links, phone numbers and addresses to the resources so that you know where to look when building your own worship song and media libraries. In this information you will find listed the most notable examples within the following types of resource category, each relating to the Songs & Media focus of this edition of the Ultimate Worship Resource Guide. For those seeking to acquire new worship songs, the following kinds of sources are included:

- Online Song Sources
- Software/Digital Files
- Periodical/Continuity clubs
- Physical Products
- Musician Instructional Resources

The second major section of this guide includes some references for those of you seeking to acquire new worship related media, both as online items or as physical items. We evaluate the following three main types of media resources:

- Online Media/Image Sites
- Physical Media/Image Sources
- Song-based Media/Image Products

More

This guide is a living document. In other words, it can and should change over time. However, each printing of it cannot be updated in hard copy – it would have to be an entirely online resource for such updates to occur. Yet the purpose of the guide is to be a "hold-in-your-hand" companion, not another online tool that gets lost in your string of endless book marks and searches. So, we have chosen to print the guide and believe it has more value to you that way. However, we recognize that the information in the guide can, and does change. We have provided for this by allowing you access to a unique website that is useful as a companion to this book. For more information about the website and how to access it, refer to page 153 and the Appendix.

How To Use This Guide

This guide is designed to be used repeatedly, as you and your church's needs change throughout the year. A first time reader will have different needs and uses for the guide than someone who is returning to use the guide for a research session to find more resources.

First Time Readers of The Guide

If this is your first time reading through this guide, please consider reading through the front sections, which include information on worship music resource history, an explanation of the resource reviews, and an explanation of the rating system. Each of these sections will help you understand how to use this guide well. The history section, especially, will give you a larger framework for worship resources – an understanding which may help place your own local church's needs and changes within the context of the extensive transition occurring across the broader church.

Experienced Readers of The Guide

Once you have used the guide, you can skip directly to the appropriate section of reviews that will help you research and acquire the songs or media content you need.

Researching Songs

For ease of use, we have divided the songs portion of this guide into two specific sections:

a) New Song Discovery: those who are looking for newly released songs (just released from songwriters, publishers and record labels),

b) Song Acquisition: those who are looking to acquire resources for specific songs. You will most likely already know the name of the songs and you just need to know the best places to acquire the resources.

New Song Discovery

If you are doing New Song Discovery, we have identified some resources that specialize in bringing fresh new content to churches in the section:

• *Where To Find New Songs: Search and Discover* (this section begins on Page 63)

Understand that you may find promotions of new songs in other locations as well. In fact, some of the website resources found in the Song Acquisition section will also be promoting new songs. The reason we have identified this separately here for new song discovery is for those who already have developed libraries of songs and want to find fresh new songs to augment their current repertoire.

Once you know what songs you are looking for, and wish to purchase or access, there is an abundance of sources to acquire resources. We have a few sections for you to consider in your search, each with several resource reviews. Depending on what type of resource you would like to acquire your songs through (online, physical product, continuity club etc), these sections will accommodate your needs:

- *Where To Acquire Songs: Online Access And Purchase* (section begins on Page 71)
- *Software/Digital Files Song Sources* (section begins on Page 85)
- *Continuity Clubs – Contemporary Song Sources* (section begins on Page 93)
- *Continuity Clubs – Choral Song Sources* (section begins on Page 99)
- *Printed/Physical Product Song Sources* (section begins on Page 105)
- *Music Instructional Resources For Song Learning* (section begins on Page 117)

Media resources are divided into three main types of categories, each containing several reviews. The categories are:

- *Online Media/Image Sites* (section begins on Page 123)
- *Physical Media/Image Sources* (section begins on Page 143)
- *Song-Based Media/Image Products* (section begins on Page 147)

The Development of Modern Worship Music Resources: Impacts of History, Style, Promotion & Technology

While this book deals directly with many specifics aspects of resources related to music and media, my reason for serving the church in worship resources is deeper than music and products. The goal of resourcing the church, for me, is to see it become captured with its holy passion once again – a fervent, world-changing love of God. It has always been my goal to resource the church, and thereby to see the church change the world.

If you are interested in understanding more about the development of worship music in the last 40 years and how that change impacted church music resources, read on. If you would rather get right to the reviews and research, feel free to jump immediately to page 59 and read about "The Rating System" that we use in our reviews and the reviews themselves, which follow thereafter.

In the journey of resourcing the local church, we can learn much by looking at the brief history of changes that have taken place in the last 40 years – a timeframe in which church music has changed considerably. These changes are important to review, since they directly impact the music, media and resources that have been in a constant state of flux for the last three decades. It is not enough for us to a simply recognize that church music style has been changing, but one must also recognize that the methodology for implementing church music has changed drastically for the leaders and musicians involved in the worship services in local churches.

If the change in style and methodologies in our musical liturgy were not enough transition, technological advancement would guarantee change to our local churches and ministries. While cultural changes were impacting music and style in the church, science and technological changes also began to exert their influence on our local churches.

Lastly, the way in which songs would become popularized for local church use has changed drastically as well in the aforementioned three decades.

These four things: the historical change in music style (across the decades of the 60s through present); the change in the popular liturgical music tools and methodology; the technological changes in music and media; and the change in promotional channels for popularizing worship songs are the areas we will cover. These areas of change simultaneously impacted and transformed church worship music and media. Each of these is dealt with in this following section.

The view presented here is reflective of my particular expertise and fields of work – church music resourcing and technology. Through a series of circumstances (and, I believe, God's direction), I have had the unique opportunity to participate in a number of different professional fields that stretched across the gambit of change that was occurring in local church worship and music ministries.

As a music industry insider, local church worship leader, professional technologist and business leader, I had the privilege of having contact with literally tens of thousands of churches in the last 15 years.

A word of clarity – while the perspective presented (mine) is specifically attuned to what has happened in church worship and music ministries, it does not reflect a complete survey of all Christian church music or all traditions, and is most certainly

North American in focus. That said, since I have dealt with such a large number of churches for so many years, I believe this fairly represents the impact and changes that praise and worship music (later called just worship music) has made across the broader church in the last 3 decades.

Worship music (as a musical sub-genre) became popular in the 1980s, when Christian music publishers such as Maranatha Music, Integrity Music and Vineyard Music started releasing recordings of songs meant for use in local churches, as distinct from the general Christian music category of CCM (Contemporary Christian Music). Worship music was typified by first person language, with lyrics directed toward God from the congregant, and it featured a simple, melodic, choral music format. The musical roots of the genre started long before the 1980s, but the term "worship music" was not used until then.

Worship music was more than just a change in terminology from hymns. The content of lyrics and music took on many popular musical idioms and often personalized the message of the songs to focus on a deeper *worship experience* and intimacy with God. The original moniker of praise music eventually became praise and worship music, and finally has become simply "worship music." All the phrases have become virtually synonymous today. Implicit in early definitions was that *praise* music was usually used to refer to faster, upbeat type of songs, while *worship* music would imply slower, more pensive expressions of adoration and worship to God. While these are not the biblical definitions of those words, they became de-facto definitions for many, due greatly to the labeling of products by music companies.

The term "worship music" did not come into use as a common expression until the mid-90s. The etymology of the phrase is really a progression from the original coined phrase of "praise music," which began appearing and being labeled as such during the early 1970s. This expression was an outgrowth of the music ministries that accompanied the Jesus People movement of the 70s through the US especially as it originated from the Calvary Chapel churches throughout Southern California. The Jesus people also concurrently expanded the notion of popular Christian music with *Jesus music*, which eventually became known as CCM (Contemporary Christian Music).

Much of the original praise music was itself heavily inspired by a series of then "contemporized" church songs written from the lyrics of the Bible, called "Scripture in Song." Those songs were written by David and Dale Garratt of New Zealand and served to ignite music in Calvary Chapel churches (which became Maranatha Music) and other groups worldwide.

Maranatha Music was the main purveyor of the "praise music" label, and carries that banner even today. Songs such as the classic "I Love You, Lord" and "Seek Ye First" became the anthems to an entire generation of believers who came to Christ during this time. Corresponding with the growth of praise music within North American churches, the UK was also churning through cultural shift, and worship leader/songwriter Graham Kendrick emerged as an early influential voice in songwriting for the new "church music" liturgy.

Toward the late 70s and at the start of the 80s, another southern California church-based music group began expanding in popularity – Vineyard Music. Springing up from the music ministries of the Vineyard churches, they reflected very similar style and lyrical content as the early Calvary Chapel/Maranatha Music song content, but began to label their songs as "worship songs." In the mid 80s other companies sprang up to meet the needs of the quickly modernizing church. Musical tastes and styles were rapidly changing as the church struggled to close a gap of nearly fifty years from the modern music of the culture. The 70s, 80s and 90s saw the church close that gap with increasing attentiveness to modern sounds and expressions.

In 1987, a music ministry that birthed "Hosanna Music" began to expand. Originally as direct mail club, eventually changing its name to Integrity Music, they branded the phrase "praise worship" into their products, solidifying the moniker for many church music lovers. Over the next 5-10 years, songwriters and worship leaders such as Don Moen, Ron Kenoly, Kent Henry, Bob Fitts, Lynn Deshazo, Gary Sadler, Daniel Gardner, Billy Funk, Marty Nystrom, Lenny LeBlanc and many other writers worked with producer Tom Brooks and helped fill American churches with new choruses that became the basis of the Integrity song catalog.

Integrity Music would eventually become the largest of the original three "praise & worship" publishers (Integrity, Maranatha and Vineyard). Integrity had a deep impact in denominational churches with its broad musical pallet which included choral musicals (Don Moen), gospel/R&B (Ron Kenoly) and children's worship (Miss Pattycake & the Donut Man) music.

As the 90s came along, Vineyard Music had expanded as well, and became very popular during the 1994-1998 time frame, when a corresponding revitalization in their churches birthed a plethora of still well-used songs throughout the global church. During that time, Vineyard almost completely labeled its music "Worship Music." It was also during that time that UK influences from modern sounds of worship bands like Delirious?, and writers such as Matt Redman began to appear. Birthed out of the Soul Survivor youth movement in the UK, these writers formed centrally under the Kingsway Music brand, many of whom gave direct acknowledgement regarding their stylistic inspiration and philosophical roots to Vineyard Music writers such as Kevin Prosch and others. After its distribution success with Vineyard Music during the mid 90s, EMI Christian Music Group brought the UK worship of Redman and Delirious? (and others in the Kingsway family) into the North American strata, through the brand "WorshipTogether." The brand grew from 1998 until the present with names such as Delirious?, Matt Redman, Tim Hughes and others.

The 90s also saw a global contribution in church music from Hillsong Australia songwriters and worship leaders writing songs that would sweep the world with popularity and longevity as anthems of the modern church. Originally with worship leaders and songwriters Geoff Bullock, and later Darlene Zschech, Hillsong eventually became the most recognized church community in modern worship songwriting.

In 1994, the first online discussion group appeared related to worship and music (called the "Worship List"). It quickly expanded into a community website called "praise.net" and survives to this day as the oldest online information center on the topic. Out of that online community, the first online worship and music resource (WorshipMusic.com) was started in 1998.

Popularity And Airplay: 2000 & beyond

The popularity of worship music has grown tremendously since the year 2000, and has seen the release of many new worship music albums by both the major record companies and independent labels. Once relegated to congregational singing only, this explosion brought worship music to the forefront of the Christian music market.

At the turn of the century, some seminal recordings impacted church music greatly. Three of the most influential of those recordings were *Hungry* (Vineyard UK), *Sonicflood* (CCM pop renditions of popular worship songs) and Michael W. Smith's first *Worship* album, all of which expanded the praise and worship genre's influence into every strata of Christian music.

One of the vanguards of church music in the first decade of the 21st century has been the college-age Passion movement (and the sixsteps Records label which was birthed from it) in the United States, which mimicked the form and success of Soul Survivor and Kingsway Music in the UK during the late 90s. Passion conference worship leaders Chris Tomlin, David Crowder, Charlie Hall and others forged ahead to bring worship music into broad popularity through songs which not only took over Sunday mornings at church, but the airwaves of radio stations formerly dedicated only to Christian pop music.

While Michael W. Smith and other Christian pop groups had made CCM styled versions of many 90s worship songs, Chris Tomlin and writers Matt Redman and Tim Hughes were writing the songs that became the staple of thousands of Christian radio stations and hundreds of thousands of churches. Along with the continued influence of the Hillsong writers from Australia, popular gospel artist/worship leader Israel Houghton and American songwriter Paul Baloche, the modern church hymn writers for the new millennium were continuing to update the repertoire of local churches everywhere.

Traditional to Popular

Moving away from organizations and people related to church music in the last three decades, the origin of contemporary worship music was also the result of a broad shift in musical styles. This change in style was not distinct (nor could it be) from its implementation in local churches. Playing different music required different instruments and methodologies. This change was typified by a shift away from 19th and 20th century classical and traditional forms of musical liturgy which involved largely piano and choir-based, multi-part vocal applications in its songs. The transition was made to a style that matched the musical and vocal nuances of popular music as it was developing from the mid 60s until the present day. Originating from campfire songs with the sound of 60s folk music stylings, these simple songs were easily played by musicians and easily learned and sung by the congregants of churches in which they were played.

Critics and proponents of older church music styles (such as hymnal traditionalists) have criticized the more modern musical style of worship music as being lyrically simplistic. Some even believed that updating the musical style of church music was somehow denigrating to the sacredness of the old forms of chants, hymns and traditionally prescribed songs often assigned for use in many Christian denominations.

This conflict between church music traditionalists and modern church music proponents became popularized in the last 20 years as the "worship wars," which encompassed a broader set of issues but was typified by the stylistic differences of musical genres held by the varying parties.

But church music did change, and the more popular sounds of folk and rock music became a norm of the new worship music style.

The Worship Service's Changing M.O.

Worship music not only brought a shift of musical style into the church, it forced a change in the *tools* and the *people* needed to play the music. Traditional and classical forms of worship music often required classically trained musicians (centered, often, on the piano) and choral singers with multi-part vocal harmonization skills (SATB). The new worship music changed this by utilizing:

- the acoustic guitar,
- simple, melodic song writing,
- garage band musicians and ensemble formats,
- and the chord chart.

These changes in the way church music was learned, played and disseminated had a dramatic effect on the musical liturgy of the Christian church in the modern western world.

The Acoustic Guitar

The introduction of the acoustic guitar as a new primary instrument made the music portable and accessible in almost any venue, where the previous piano-based liturgy was limited to church sanctuaries, meeting places and a few homes. This shift alone helped this new church music to mirror the wildfire spread of popular music that happened throughout the last half of the 20th century, when the influence of the guitar dominated the cultural strata of music in North America and Europe.

Simple, Melodic Songwriting

The predominance of simple, melodic writing in songs was an early earmark of this music. This diverged from the extensive and almost exclusive use of SATB choral applications for vocal parts, which had predated worship music. This new simplicity contributed greatly to the musical style's popularity among congregants who found the music infectious and memorable, also mirroring pop music's influence through the 20th century.

Garage Band Musicians

A corollary factor in the musical style change included the extensive use of non-classically trained musicians (garage band and self-taught musicians) in congregations which espoused worship music. Propelling this was the introduction not only of popular music styles, but the huge influx of tens of thousands of "hippies" (converted through the Jesus people movement of the 60s and 70s) into churches across America. With them, and the growing popular music culture in the US, garage band musicians poured into churches.

The Chord Chart

The use of the chord chart as a common method of transcribing, distributing and learning new songs came to fruition inside the church with the praise and worship revolution. Originating from the popular use of fake books in folk music and general music culture, chord charts also moved in to the church. With the use of chord charts in the 90s, church music began to be shared and distributed quickly. Much to the chagrin of the church music publishers, this was accelerated by the use of photocopying in the 90s, then by the instant reach of the internet after the turn of the century.

This is not to say the chord chart has overtaken use of standard piano and vocal scores in the church. Those formats remain very much alive. As worship music has matured in its form, the musical style has actually become more complex in the last 15 years, in contrast to its early very simple forms in the 70s and 80s. The use of chord charts will continue to flux as the music form evolves.

The change in musical style and methodology was relatively easy to measure from one perspective – church resource sales. As churches moved from traditional style hymns to popular choruses of the 80's, then praise and worship songs of the 90s, and modern worship anthems in the last 10 years, those changes were reflected in what churches purchased for their worship ministries.

Hymnals did not disappear completely, but the transition to lyric-based song aids for the congregation ushered in a new era in worship for churches the world over. For over two hundred years the hymnal was the guardian of Protestant church music for both the members of the congregations it served and the ministers who employed it. The hymnal's supplanting dispersed its responsibilities in two ways – church members moved away from its use as a lyrical guide and ministers moved away from its use as a musical source.

Church congregations began to use projection screens (and later video screens) to follow the songs of the modern liturgy. This began with overhead transparencies (in the 70s and 80s), slide projection (in the late 80s and early 90s), TV screen projection (only by larger churches in mid-late the 90s), and eventually (by 2000) software-driven computer displays using software specifically built for lyric presentation. By the end of the millennial decade (2010), the majority of churches in North America had begun using some form of multimedia presentation system.

During this same time, church musicians and leaders began to use modern songbooks, lead sheets, chord charts, even Nashville Number System charts as musician resources. This began in the form of large collections that largely mimicked the hymnal predecessors' gathering of hundreds of popular songs, only this was filled with praise and worship choruses. *Maranatha Red Book*, *Maranatha Green Book*, *More Songs for Praise and Worship*, *Integrity's Hosanna* volumes and *Vineyard's Songs of the Vineyard* were examples of songbooks that mimicked the hymnal format of large collections of songs.

Those large collections became unwieldy and expensive as the pace of music introduction quickened (with the popularity of worship music growing through the late 80s through mid 90s). Churches began to rely more on continuity clubs during this time, garnering music resources from *Integrity's Hosanna* club, *Vineyard's Touching the Father's Heart* series, and the continued *Maranatha Praise* series. These were supported by a technology shift from cassette to CD audio.

By the end of the 20th century, the internet was in full swing. Access to legal and illegal digital copies of music was exploding. Onstage audio, online purchasing of gear, cheaper digital mixing equipment and other technology changes were propelling the church music ministries into a digital age.

While most musicians were not getting their new song repertoire exclusively from the internet, any audio music resource was quickly accessible online (legally or illegally). Collections of musician resources were soon sold in digital formats (PDFs online, CD-ROMs with vast libraries and software programs with musical tools). In 2001, WorshipTogether.com began releasing online "how-to" videos allowing members to view instructional "New Song Café" episodes which explained how to play new songs. By 2005, YouTube had launched its popular video streaming service. In less than two years the internet provided a huge collection of "how-to" videos (on YouTube and others), allowing instant access to learn songs quickly by the large and growing contingent of non-classically trained musicians that filled the volunteer and paid ranks of church music ministries.

What happened in three decades (80s, 90s and 2000s) is that both the church musicians and church members quickly incorporated changes in media and music technology to facilitate their needs in the worship context. While the strict use of a hymnal remains in place in some churches, its inflexibility as a tool for local churches ultimately became the cause of its demise, in the face of technological solutions which completely transformed the church ministry tool set and the congregational worship experience.

While there are many benefits to having the flexibility afforded by technology, it is clear (and can be seen clearly on page 54 in *Figure 1 – Forty Years of Church Music Resources*) that the fragmentation of church worship resources into so many components has ironically become as painful in its complexity as the hymnal was in its inflexibility.

While this was relatively clear to see for someone involved in church music resources, it was painfully unclear to many entertainment music labels who tried, often unsuccessfully, to sell products into the "church music" resource world in the last 15 years.

Despite their misunderstanding of the church music resource market, entertainment music labels (and the Christian pop artists on their rosters) would eventually gain influence in bringing new worship songs to the church through the use of radio, as we will see in the next section.

Changes in Promotional Channels for Songs

The last major shift in church music that was occurring in the previous three decades was the way in which new songs reached the local congregations.

The Hymnal As The Song Source

Since the Protestant Reformation, books of liturgy and prayer grew up connected to specific denominational groups. Hymns were no different. They were prescribed through the tradition you belonged to, and the release of a new hymnal volume was a major undertaking for both publishers and churches.

For generations of Christian worshipers the hymnal provided the lyrical guide for congregants, the music source for the musicians (mostly piano), and the song source for leaders developing their repertoire. The changes that accompanied modern worship forced the functions embodied by the hymnal to be disseminated into several different functions, as can be seen in *Figure 1 – Forty Years of Church Music Resources* on page 54.

Word Of Mouth

With the advent of popularized worship music, from the 70s forward, the minister's reliance on the hymnal as the repertoire for the local church began to change. Through most of the 70s and 80s much of the popularization of new songs came simply through word of mouth. One remembers songs like "Change My Heart O God" (by Eddie Espinosa) or even parts of songs, like the chorus of "Awesome God" (by Rich Mullins) making it to local churches by a friend's recommendation. The great songs spread like wild fire through the tinder dry American church.

Early Continuity Clubs And Events

By the early 90s each of the three major worship music publishers (Integrity, Maranatha and Vineyard) were capable recording and publishing organizations. The advent of digital audio (CDs) and other technologies allowed recordings to improve so that live settings gave good demonstrations of the newest songs. Continuity clubs proliferated new songs to the churches through regular releases of new albums with corresponding songbooks. These clubs became the new repertoire song source for churches.

The popularity of continuity clubs waned in the late 90s when the best new songs began appearing in separately released projects, such as *Worship Together's Revival Generation* series. By this time, the use of internet marketing (via its WorshipTogether.com site) and touring events had become a primer for new songs, as Worship Together rose to promote the songs of the writers from Passion, Kingsway UK and other EMI labels.

Radio Writes the Playlist

With the popularity of worship music reaching its apex in the first five years of the 21st century, CCM artists Michael W. Smith, Sonicflood, Third Day, Chris Tomlin and others had driven the songs to popular Christian radio. This signaled the most recent shift in the source of new songs for church repertoires – Christian radio.

Music Industry Struggles

During the first decade of the 21st century, the music industry (including the Christian and worship music genres) became the first media victim of the internet age. A number of companies involved have imploded or merged. The music industry found itself under siege from rampant illegal copying and downloading of songs. Soon, revenues were evaporating and financial statements were hemorrhaging red ink. Previously large music companies were now remnant staffs servicing only the most popular artists and repertoire.

Some companies are still producing resources but only for a few remaining very popular brand names such as Hillsong and Chris Tomlin, which continue to garner significant exposure through radio play of their songs.

Recently, some music has become popular through association with influential church ministries, such as Bethel Church's Jesus Culture music, New Life Colorado's worship department, Kansas City's IHOP /the Call events and a few large national conferences around North America such as Passion events.

While websites and online marketing continue to promote new worship songs, these are not as broadly impacting on their own. Christian radio, along with popular brands/influential ministries, continues to be more effective in supplying new songs to North American churches.

How The Hymnal Was Replaced

"Why does all this history matter?" you may ask. Hopefully, the answer is now clear to you. This change has had a crucial impact on worship and music resources.

It is clear that four major areas of change have altered church music and resources irrevocably:

- **Style**: historical change in music style – hymns to popular music
- **Methods**: change in liturgical music tools and methodology – piano and choirs gave way to guitar-driven rock bands
- **Tools**: technological changes in music and media – hymnals to computer driven screens for the congregation and digital PDF sheet music and online audio for the musicians
- **Repertoire Source**: change in promotional channels for popularizing new songs – hymnals gave way to continuity clubs, popular events, and eventually Christian radio as the promotional vehicle for songs to the local church.

As the following diagram illustrates, each one of these areas was previously governed by the hymnal. As we have said, the hymnal was the lyric source for congregations. This has now changed to computer drive video screens (and software). The hymnal once was the music source for the organist or pianist. That changed to

51

separate musician songbooks and collections, and is now PDF sheet music and online resources. The hymnal was once the source for songs in developing a local church repertoire. This has now changed to radio (and some internet promotion).

With the development of modern worship, much of the hymnal functions were replaced by a number of other resources. The result was an explosion of need in worship resources. With so many resources available, it soon became confusing for churches to understand how to make good decisions on which resources were best for them.

It is out of that need that this book has been written. My hope is that the pages of this book help to save you time and money in searching for the resources you may need for your local church.

Much of what we have explored in these sections explains how the hymnal has been replaced by other tools as the primary worship resource of most churches. This does not mean the hymnal is gone or is without value. In fact, for churches that choose to use the hymnal, it can be a simplifying, helpful resource that rids them of the complexities of many "modern" solutions.

The following diagram details the transition through the recent decades for many churches. One benefit of viewing the changes in worship resources this way is that it allows us to see how the functions of the hymnal dispersed into the various online, digital and media resources that exist today.

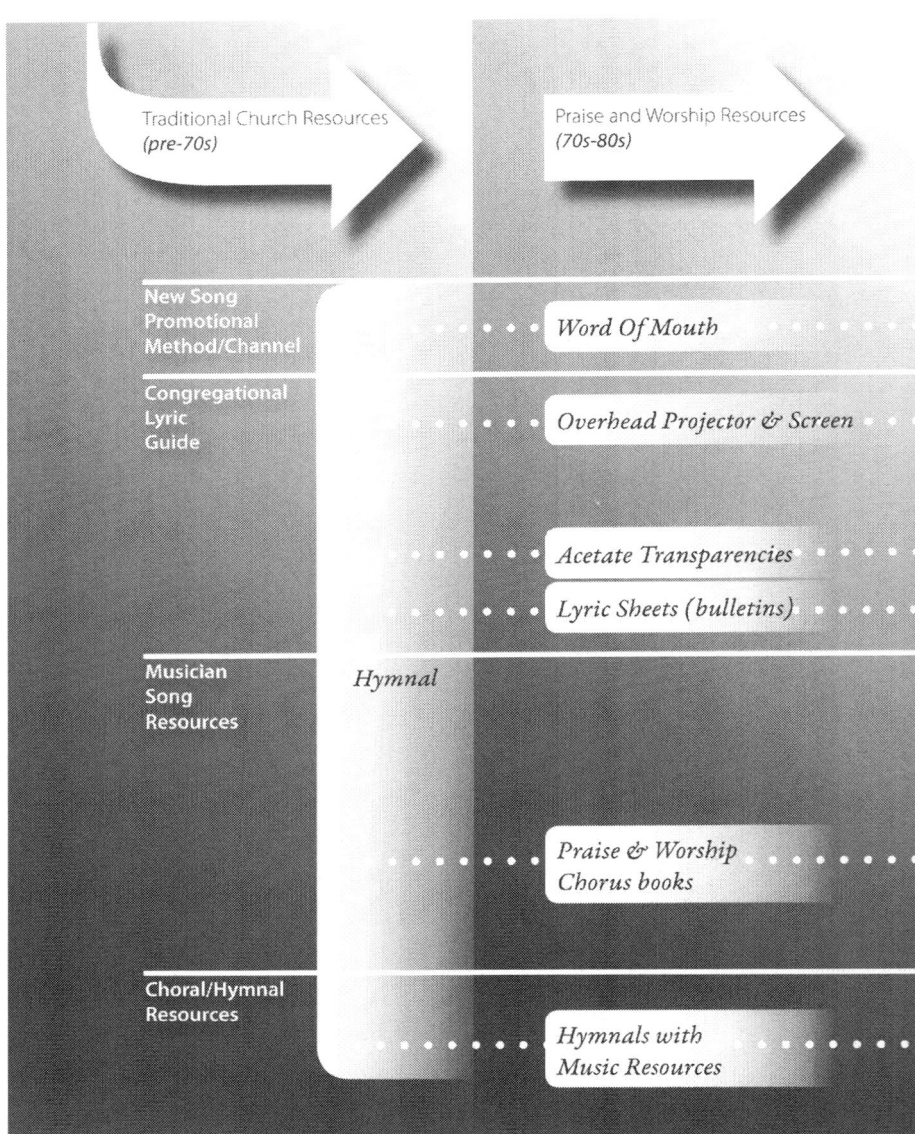

Figure 1 – Forty Years of Church Music Resources

Worship Resources (90s)	Modern Resources (2000- present)
Events & Continuity Clubs	Brand Names & Christian Radio
Slide & TV Projection	Computer Driven Displays
Lyric Slides	Presentation Software
	Digital Lyric Sources
Lyric Sheets (bulletins)	Multimedia backgrounds
CDs & Accompanying Songbooks	Popular Collections (WorshipTogether, iWorship)
	Online Audio (MP3s, etc.)
	Online PDF Lead Sheets and charts
Music and Worship Software	Online Chord Chart/Music Services
Choral Packages (CD, Trax, Arrangements)	Digital Hymnals & Software
	Web-based Hymn Arrangements

This guide contains over 100 reviews. Each review has seven possible components to it:

- **Resource Title** – the name of the website, service or product.

- **Rating** – a rating from 1-5 stars (see page 59 for more details on "The Rating System").

- **Review Text** – a text summary of the review, highlighting the most important aspects of the resource from our perspective.

- **URL** – a web link to the resource. In some cases, this will be the full URL. For printing considerations, some URLs have been shortened (using *bit.ly* or *amzn.to*).

- **Review ID** – an ID code for the review. You can use this ID to locate the review links on the guide website (see the "Appendix: Ultimate Worship Resource Guide – Online Tools" on page 153 for more information).

- **Telephone** – where applicable, a phone contact has been included.

- **Mailing Address** – where applicable, a mailing address has been included.

The guide contains a rating system used throughout. You will see one of the following ratings for each individual listing. Please note that these ratings are based on the opinions of this reviewer. You may disagree with them. In general, we feel that they represent a common-sense summation of the quality of the resource at this time. Your personal experience may vary, of course. At the very least, we think these evaluations can help you notice the highest ranked resources as ones to consider in your search.

☆☆☆☆☆ 0 stars – This resource has little or no value relative to the use for which it is commissioned or marketed.

★☆☆☆☆ 1 star – This resource has some nominal value, but lacks significant content, function or interface to adequately serve the user.

★★☆☆☆ 2 stars – This resource has value. However, it lacks breadth of content, function or interface, especially in light of other resources that are available. You might find some gems here, but the site does not help you find them, or it is sparse in its overall selection.

59

 3 stars – This resource has good content and a reasonable interface. People find it useful, and it continues to be an ongoing source of value. Most resources fall into this category rating.

 4 stars – This resource has excellent content, good application and strong interface. People regularly refer to this resource as a mainstay in its category, or a leader in some aspect of its use (quality, search, function).

 5 stars – The absolute best. Few resources get this designation. This resource provides not only breadth of content and exceptional quality, but is clearly the leader in its aspect of ministry. What it does, it does as well or better than any other resource.

The goal of this book is to save you time and money, allowing you to find and purchase the resources you need. This book contains over 100 reviews of the top resources that we believe are worth spending money on. Of those 100+ resources, very few get 5 stars and the ones that do are exceptional. To highlight them, we list them below for your convenience. They are listed in alphabetical order.

- Corbis Images (website)
- Dan Stevers (website)
- HymnCharts.com (website)
- iWorship Flexx (product)
- iWorship MPEG Video Library (product)
- Nooma Films (website)
- PraiseCharts.com (website)
- The Praise And Worship Song Book/ CD-Rom Edition (product)
- WorshipHouseMedia.com (website)
- WorshipTeam.com (website)
- X.0: The Digital Hymnal for the Modern Worship Generation (product)

Where To Find New Songs: Search and Discover

Below are sources that we believe are some of the best places for you to find and hear about new songs. Many of these locations are meant just for that – research and discovery of songs for your church needs. You may find good new songs at these sites, although it is likely you will have to use the "Online Song Access and/or Purchase" section to find the best places to actually buy or access usable resources for songs in your church, once you have found the songs you like. The following are some examples of notable entities that offer great research capabilities, good "new song" features, or are popular places for new songs. Also note that you should review the separate section for continuity clubs (later in this guide) which can also be an excellent source for new songs, although often specific to individual publishers.

WorshipTogether.com is the promotional site for all EMI-CMG artists and songs. For over 10 years this site has been the icon of song introduction to the modern church in America. It still holds a prominent position and is the first stop for many people looking for new songs. Popular for a lot of artists like Chris Tomlin, Passion, Hillsong United, David Crowder, Tim Hughes, Matt Redman, Starfield, Brenton Brown, Audrey Assad, Gungor, Leeland and others. They regularly have new song features and artist information. WorshipTogether.com is from this very popular group of writers and artists.

It is a free site and but requires membership for some features. The site has been cleaned up recently, looks better and operates more smoothly than in previous years. It has links to other sites for purchasing, but you are not able to buy anything directly on WorshipTogether.com itself.

URL: http://www.worshiptogether.com

Review: **SM1**

★★★★☆

IntegritySongs.com is the marketing site for all Integrity/Vertical/Hosanna artists and songs. This is a relatively new site that draws together many  previous resources and people from brands like Vertical Music, Hosanna, Global Worship Now, Gateway, New Life Worship and other groups. This site is a popular resource for information on artists like Paul Baloche, Brian Doerksen, Gateway Church, Israel Houghton, John Mark McMillan, Jared Anderson, Lincoln Brewster, Kari Job, Kathryn Scott, Ken Reynolds, Paul Wilbur and others. They regularly have new song features and artist information. Also includes associated videos, blogs, promotions and other information. It is a free site but requires membership for some features. It has links to other sites for purchasing, but you are not able to buy anything directly on IntegritySongs.com itself. This site is linked to its Facebook presence where integrated e-cards and features are released regularly.

URL: http://www.integritysongs.com
Review: **SM2**

★★★★★

WorshipTeam.com is a worship planner filled with legal songs from all of the major worship publishers.

WorshipTeam.com *adds new songs weekly*, making it a great place to constantly check out new songs being released. While it already includes over 6000 legal worship songs (and growing) preloaded into the WorshipTeam.com song database with lyrics, chord charts and full-length audio, it adds new releases from publishers and labels such as Vineyard Music USA/UK, Integrity Music, Word Music (Fervent, Word, Myrrh), Vertical Music, Hillsong Australia, EMI CMG (sixsteps, Sparrow, Worshiptogether), Kingsway Music UK, INO Records, Jesus Culture/Bethel Music, Ardent Records, Sovereign Grace Music, ION Worship, Alletrop, ShadowSpring, LenSongs and several others included in the WorshipTeam.com content.

Especially helpful is the "New Songs" tab in WorshipTeam.com which shows you a reverse chronological list of the newest content added to the service for its users.

More information about WorshipTeam.com is available in the Song Purchase and Access section of this guide. More details, demos, screen shots, FAQs, and more can be found at

URL: http://www.worshipteam.com
Review: **SM3**

CCLI TV is an online video site run by Christian Copyright Licensing International. CCLI TV  has three sections, but as a "new song" source, only two of them apply. First, they have "Open Mic," which is a collection of videos that show new songs releasing from churches. Most videos are live worship sessions featuring the new song. The goal is for you to hear fresh new songs that are well done and being used in local churches. Second, CCLI TV has a channel called "First Take." This is a collection of new songs that are promoted by major worship publishers, allowing you to see (again video examples) of the songs and hear them done well. Both these services of CCLI TV are free and do not require you to have a login to view.

> URL: http://www.ccli.com/CCLITV
> Review: **SM4**

> Telephone: (800) 234-2446
> Mailing address: CCLI
> 17201 NE Sacramento Street,
> Portland, OR 97230

SongQuery.com is just that – a search engine and directory of tens of thousands of songs and over 10,000 products. It does not sell anything, but is an effective a way to find a specific song or artist or product. Its usefulness is to help you locate what product a given song is on. In that way, it is great for the search process. It is a free site and has no membership or fee or such – it is just a search directory. It has links to Amazon for purchasing.

> URL: http://www.songquery.com
> Review: **SM5**

Digital Worship News

Digital Worship News is an online newsletter (both email and web) with regular reviews of new projects, songs and releases. Subscription is free. It currently has over 80,000 subscribers and is one of the largest, most popular of such online publications.

> URL: http://www.digitalworshipnews.com/dwn
> Review: **SM6**

SongDiscovery is from Worship Leader magazine. It comes out several times a year bundled with an issue of the magazine. It includes 12-15 songs, PowerPoint & MediaShout files, chord charts and lead sheets in 3 keys, scripture and theme references.

URL: http://www.songdiscovery.com/subscribe
Review: **SM7**

Telephone toll free: (888) 881-5861
Mailing address: Song Discovery
32234 Paseo Adelanto, Ste. A
San Juan Capistrano, CA 92675

Kim Gentes Reviews

For over 15 years, I have written reviews on new music and worship resources. They are effective and church resource focused. Over 60 reviews of various worship projects and resources.

URL: http://bit.ly/fh6AIW (Music Reviews)
URL: http://bit.ly/fcnNuM (Resource reviews)
Review: **SM8**

Finding and researching songs is not enough. To use songs in your local church, you will need sources that allow for legal access to online versions of songs or purchase of the songs and resources. In this section, we have listed what we believe are the best sources for you to access and purchase those songs. The examples are notable entities that offer a large selection of worship songs available for purchase or access online. You will note that in this section we only list sites that allow you to acquire legal song content. We do not list sites that illegally allow access to sheet music, chord charts or MP3s that are used without the permission and licensing of the publishers/labels. All sources listed here are legal in that regard, according to our review of the site and checking with the music companies for verification.

WorshipTeam.com

★★★★★

WorshipTeam.com is an online worship planning service, with tools for your entire worship ministry. This includes giving you legal access  to both chord charts/lyrics and full length audio to thousands of worship songs (including the latest). You can print off chord charts and lyrics, and play full length audio of any song from its database of over 6000 worship songs (and growing) which are preloaded into its song database.

Includes publishers and labels such as Vineyard Music USA/UK, Integrity Music, Word Music (Fervent, Word, Myrrh), Vertical Music, Hillsong Australia, EMI CMG (sixsteps, Sparrow, Worshiptogether), Kingsway Music UK, INO Records, Jesus Culture/Bethel Music, Ardent Records, and dozens of others. Song lyrics are instantly exportable to Media Shout, EasyWorship, ProPresenter and other display software databases.

While WorshipTeam.com provides songs with its service, songs are just one of its components. It is a complete planner, with scheduling, and other features. Pricing varies by the size of your worship team, and the first month is free. Canceling the service at any time is a simple and a pain free experience. Details, free trial, FAQs, and more found at:

URL: http://www.worshipteam.com
Review: **SM9**

★ ★ ★ ★ ★

PraiseCharts.com (sheet music and praise band arrangements)  offers thousands of individual worship songs available for online download purchase via their web site. For their song titles, they have written lyrics, chord charts, lead sheets, worship choir charts, praise band arrangements, jazz band arrangements, and full orchestrations available. Plus, they have a wide range of audio tracks to complement the charts.

PraiseCharts has been *the undisputed leader of the print music arrangement category for modern worship songs* and has recently added the entire catalog of one of the other providers in the online worship music genre (WordMusicNow) to its site. Absolutely worth checking out.

> URL: http://www.praisecharts.com
> Review: **SM10**

> Phone: (800) 695-6293
> Mailing address: PraiseCharts
> Suite 123 #505-8840 210th Street
> Langley, BC V1M 2Y2 / Canada

HymnCharts is the brain child of its owner/arranger Don Chapman. It is part of the larger network of sites called HeartsToGod.com. Don's passion with HymnCharts.com comes out clearly because he provides just one thing – and does that very well – *the best contemporary arrangements and resources for using a large collection of hymns* in modern service contexts. The selection of hymns is strong (over 100 completely arranged titles), but what is most impressive is his complete rendering of arrangements for each selection. Literally 14 different arrangement components for each hymn are available (everything you would need in any church context). HymnCharts is unique in that it sticks just to hymns, and that makes it easily the best resource anywhere for those wanting to get access to this great collection of arrangements. The service is simple and clear – it is an online access, monthly fee, allowing you access to the library of songs and an additional 1 new hymn arrangement added each month. While there are others who provide hymns within their catalog of songs, none focus and succeed in the world of blended and contemporary arrangement of hymns as well as HymnCharts.

URL: http://www.hymncharts.com
Review: **SM11**

Telephone: (800)761-3550
Mailing Address: HymnCharts
PO Box 232, Mauldin, SC 29662

★★★★☆

LifewayWorship.com allows users to arrange (via Songmap),  purchase, download and print flexible, music arrangements, audio MP3s, backing tracks and multi-tracks for worship teams, choirs, praise bands, and orchestras. They also have lead sheets, chord charts, Power Point lyrics, and other formats on selected songs.

The main power feature of this resource is its online drag/drop arrangement tool for audio files (called Songmap). You can *literally create an audio track by dragging and dropping components of a song* around on the screen. The audio is professional and perfect for local churches that need audio reference customized.

> URL: http://www.lifewayworship.com
> Review: **SM12**

> Phone: (800) 436-3869
> Mailing address: LifeWay Worship
> 1 LifeWay Plaza, MSN 126,
> Nashville, TN 37234-0126

DiscoverWorship.com offers both pay-as-you-go as well as subscription purchase plans (however, I believe that currently there are over twice as many songs available for subscribers than are available in their pay-as-you-go offerings). When you download a song you have purchased from their web site, you will receive all the audio tracks, charts, written lyrics, and other files bundled together in one easy ZIP file. You can also print as many copies of the sheet music as you want for your church music ministry.

URL: http://www.discoverworship.com/subscriptions
Review: **SM13**

Telephone toll free: (866) 859-7622

WordMusicNow allows users to purchase, download and print flexible, two-key single-song music arrangements of the newest and best songs for worship teams, choir, praise bands, and orchestras. Also, selected songs have lead sheets, chord charts, sheet music, written lyrics, and rhythm/vocal arrangements.

> URL: http://wordmusicnow.com
> Review: **SM14**
>
> Mailing address: Word Music
> 25 Music Square West
> Nashville, TN 37203

GreatWorshipSongs.com is an online store offering a selection of songs from Brentwood-Benson. Each song typically comes with downloadable MP3 full audio, and printable chord charts. Some songs have printable sheet music and audio accompaniment trax.

> URL: http://www.greatworshipsongs.com
> Review: **SM15**

★ ★ ★ ☆ ☆

Vineyard Resources is the online distribution arm that handles  product and resource sales direct to churches/individuals for all of Vineyard products. With Vineyard music and resources being produced in the US, UK and other locations worldwide, it is nice to see one place that has all the Vineyard material in one location. This site includes every Vineyard song, every CD, many out of print projects, plus some PDF songbooks, loop packages (for some songs) and more. If you are looking for Vineyard stuff, this is your place to go.

URL: http://www.vineyardresources.com/equip/music
Review: **SM16**

Telephone toll free: (800) 852-8463

ION Worship

ION Worship is a little known online site that represents a community of several well known leaders such Brian Doerksen, Andy Park, David Ruis, Michael Larson, Sean Dayton, Bethel Church and others. ION Worship is the defacto franchise for Vineyard music in Canada and includes the music from Vineyard including all of the US Vineyard projects. ION sells both MP3s and CDs and everything is reasonably priced.

URL: http://ionworship.org
Review: **SM17**

Kingsway Shop

Kingsway Music has a nice selection of downloadable single song sheet music, and a nice selection of songbooks. It also has a good selection of traditional hymns and contemporary-genre, sheet music and charts. Most of the music is from Kingsway and its partners. Site layout and search, though complete, is not very user friendly.

URL: http://www.kingswayshop.com
Review: **SM18**

J.W. Pepper has "e-Print Download" individual song sheet music available for hundreds of Christian worship songs and hymns. Many persons find that using their web site for the first time can be somewhat challenging when seeking the song downloads. To save you some time, you can try using the following URL to go straight to their current selection of Christian genre sheet music downloads (hint: while on the web page select the "e-Print Downloads" search filter in the left margin of the web page):

http://bit.ly/eJxZW0 (all Church music)

http://bit.ly/hfrhYn (Choir music)

Review: **SM19**

Cyber Hymnal

Cyber Hymnal has been online for about 15 years. They have over 8000 hymns and songs from many denominations. Almost exclusively public domain songs, downloads from this web site are free for anyone to access. Lyrics and sheet music scores are in NoteWorthy Composer or PDF format. This site has a poor interface, but has a vast collection of hymns with MIDI file audios, pictures, biographies, song histories, and more.

> URL: http://www.hymntime.com/tch
> Review: **SM20**

Hymnal.net

Hymnal.net has thousands of songs available, and it offers songs and hymns that are either posted with legal permission or that belong to the public domain. This site has a reasonable web interface; however the search function is problematic. Most songs on this site contain guitar and piano sheet music (melody line only) with MIDI and MP3 audio available.

> URL: http://www.hymnal.net
> Review: **SM21**

CCLI SongSelect is a fee based
online service with differing
content based on price plan (Basic

Plan, Premium Plan, Advanced Harmony Plan, and Advanced
Melody Plan). CCLI SongSelect is *only* available to "Church
Copyright License" holders (I.E. you must first pay for and own
the basic CCLI license, then you can pay for this extra service in
addition to the basic license). SongSelect subscribers can download
individual song transposable Lead Sheets, Chord Charts, and
Vocal/Hymn Sheets (SATB hymn format). Strictly speaking, the
sheet music available in SongSelect is stripped down to its core
components and is the basic representation of the song. It is not
"arranged" for your band. If you are looking for the core melody,
chords, and a 4 part harmony template then CCLI Song Select is a
strong source. SongSelect has 30-second samples to hear online to
help you confirm selected songs. More details and a video demo
can be found at:

URL: http://bit.ly/eo3ql6
Review: **SM22**

Phone: (800) 234-2446
Mailing address: CCLI
17201 NE Sacramento Street,
Portland, OR 97230

MusicNotes.com

MusicNotes.com is a popular online store that has both secular music and a large quantity of Christian worship songs and hymns available. MusicNotes.com offers downloadable single-song sheet music, and some songbooks as well. Here is their URL.

URL: http://www.musicnotes.com
Review: **SM23**

SheetMusicPlus.com

SheetMusicPlus.com is similar to MusicNotes.com, in that it is a popular online store carrying both secular and Christian worship music. SheetMusicPlus.com has downloadable single-song sheet music, and songbooks. SheetMusicPlus.com makes it a bit tedious to find the Christian section, but once you are there it is extensive. The shortened URL below will drill you into their site to start your search.

URL: http://bit.ly/eilTcH
Review: **SM24**

For over 12 years WorshipMusic.com was the premier destination for worship resources in physical format. With over 8,000 different products they covered CD, tracks, print music, hymnals, instructional DVDs, MPEG DVD-ROMs, books, MIDI and much more. In September of 2010, WorshipMusic.com became part of the Christianbook.com / CBD family. For several years CBD has been building its presence in Christian music and church resourcing, through the brand CBDTunes. With the addition of the WorshipMusic.com brand and product lines, they have become even stronger. CBD has over 180,000 different products, which includes CDs, DVDs, printed music, tracks, PDFs, MP3s and more. While CBD is always a good destination to check for the lowest price, its breadth of product sometimes makes it difficult to navigate. They have made starting your search for worship resources easier with this URL.

URL: http://www.christianbook.com/WorshipMusic
Review: **SM25**

Software/Digital Files Song Sources

Here we have listed some resources of note that contain Software/Digital Files. These are things that one purchases and then uses with a computer. These items typically contain compilations of more than 50 song titles in their respective contents. Most of these products feature PDF formatted sheet music, chord charts or lead sheets and some also include audio samples of the songs. Be sure to review them for details so you know what to expect. These are all chosen based on their application as extensive libraries of the representative songs, and provide the resource in the software or digital file format.

X.0: The Digital Hymnal for the Modern Worship Generation (DVD-ROM/Book/CD)

DVD-ROM of piano/vocal/guitar, lead sheet, and chord chart PDFs with accompanying four-color retrospective book and audio CD. Published by the folks at Worship Together.

Contained within the high-quality packaging of X.0 is a complete overview of the entire Worship Together catalog, numbering over 700 songs. Opening the textured thick-stock box reveals a full-color collector's book filled with information, photos, and interviews about some of the biggest worship songs around today; a companion CD is included containing original master recordings of all the songs discussed. Inset behind the book is a *DVD-ROM containing a whopping 719 songs from the past ten years* of Worship Together, in piano/vocal/guitar, lead sheet, and chord chart format. These PDFs are tied together by a slick, searchable, cross-indexed interface that includes all the information you could want, including theme, tempo, key, scripture reference, writers, and more. The product is available online at:

> URL: http://amzn.to/fZDBeS
> Review: **SM26**

For each song in the contents, this lead-sheet style songbook includes the printed written lyrics, a simple round-note melody line on a single treble staff line, and the guitar chord letter names, all in viewable/printable PDF file format on a disk. This fake book CD-ROM *includes over 600 worship songs* in the contents. This product is perhaps the largest digital collection of songs on a product that does not require a specialized software or viewer. Any free PDF viewer (installed on almost every computer and mobile device these days) will let you browse the immense library of this resource. If you simply need the "one" resource for the last 30 years of great praise and worship songs and you want it in lead sheet format – this product is your ticket. It does not miss any popular song dated 2001 or earlier.

Here is an example of an online vendor that has it for sale:

URL: http://amzn.to/fXENPb
Review: **SM27**

This CD-ROM Songbook disk includes printable sheet music, printable chord charts, and printable lyrics sheets for all 98 songs found in the iWorship series DVDs and CDs. It can be purchased from the publisher web page. Integrity Music has published a few dozen CD-ROM digital songbooks with printable charts and sheet music; most are album project songbooks but a few are larger compilations of songs. These CD-ROM songbooks from Integrity Music can be a little hard to find on the publisher web site; they do not seem to have a dedicated section for these items so one is relegated to sifting through all the songbooks of any format they've released. Because of that, the best thing to do is simply purchase the single volume *iWorship Digital Sheet Music Library (A-N)*.

If you love the iWorship series (and who doesn't?), this is *the complete collection of the sheet music* for that series.

The shortened URL below brings you right to the iWorship product page.

URL: http://bit.ly/ieBJEW
Review: **SM28**

Worship Together Platinum Series

Worship Together released 3 "Platinum Collection" songbooks that have a CD-ROM component. Each contains over 120 songs in their respective contents, and each includes printable sheet music, chord charts, and lyric sheets. The first two in the series are out of print, but the *Worship Together Songbook 5.0 & 6.0 Collection BK/CD* Digital Songbook is still available.

URL: http://amzn.to/g2I8Bg
Review: **SM29**

The Paul Baloche Digital Sheet Music Library CD-ROM Songbook

This CD-ROM disk includes printable sheet music, printable chord charts, and printable lyrics sheets for 75 songs written by popular worship leader Paul Baloche. Here is a web page from one online vender where it is for sale at a discount price:

URL: http://bit.ly/fZSPrw
Review: **SM30**

This is a software application that contains *over 3500 public domain hymns* in the contents. For each song in the database contents, this software allows users to transpose to any key. Users can also reorder and/or delete any verses, and users can choose to display SATB, lead sheets, or chord charts with chord names and fret diagrams. Screenshots, sample printouts, a list of song titles, pricing, and more can be found at the publisher web site at the following web page URL:

URL: http://www.musicease.com/cvhymnal.html

Review: **SM31**

★★★☆☆

Softpraise is a companion tool corresponding to the popular *Songs of Faith & Praise Hymnal*. Included in the database, the software contains all the 870+ songs from the *Songs of Faith and Praise Hymnal*. Please note that users are not able to import songs or edit existing songs, and this program does not print sheet music. It does not even print chords; it only allows users to print out the song lyrics. When used with a digital projection system, this software allows users to project the song with the SATB notes on staff lines (conventional round notes or shaped-notes). Screenshots, sample printouts, a list of song titles, pricing, and more can be found at the publisher's web site. This might not be for sale online; instead we have recently heard from users that had to place an order via telephone. This is a unique product with no competition. No other projection software exists that will display staffed notation for congregational use. However, due to the numerous limitations and difficulty purchasing, this resource only got 3 stars. Here is the company URL:

URL: http://www.softpraise.com
Review: **SM32**

Telephone number: (800) 995-2802

In this next section, we have listed some resources of certain notable Periodical/Continuity clubs. Should you be interested, each of the following entities listed below offer an enrollment subscription program with varying content and costs. These typically offer new worship songs (although some include new arrangements of previously released songs as well) that can be sent automatically to subscribers via online download or in a surface shipped package sent to a street address.

SongDiscovery is a multimedia worship resource from the publishers of *Worship Leader Magazine*; it comes to subscribers several times each year bundled with a current issue of *Worship Leader Magazine*. Each disc includes 12-15 new worship songs, Power Point & MediaShout lyric files, chord charts and lead sheets in 3 different keys, along with scripture references and song themes. Because it *gathers songs from a broad range of publishers*, this resource receives a high ranking.

> URL: http://www.songdiscovery.com/subscribe
> Review: **SM33**

> Telephone toll free: (888) 881-5861
> Mailing address: Song Discovery
> 32234 Paseo Adelanto, Ste. A
> San Juan Capistrano, CA 92675

★★★☆☆

Club Vineyard is a subscription plan that offers all the new  songs released by Vineyard Music Group, and subscribers receive shipments 3-4 times annually. Subscribers can receive just the audio CD, or they can choose to receive the audio CD, chord chart access, sheet music, and one *Inside Worship Magazine* per shipment. Vineyard Music Group has been a leader in excellent contemporary worship music for over three decades.

URL: http://bit.ly/ebIG3e
Review: **SM34**

Telephone: (800) 852-VINE (8463)
Mailing address: Club Vineyard
3727 Greenbriar Dr., Suite 119
Stafford, TX 77477

Until May, 2011 Spin 360 (SPIN) was a subscription service plan that included 10-12 songs on a volume. However, it no longer has new volumes being produced and its subscription offering has ceased. Why do we list SPIN, then? We list it because the entire set of 54 completed volumes (hundreds of songs) in the SPIN collection is still available for purchase. SPIN is primarily meant for student ministers to provide relevant praise music for today's students. SPIN's purpose is to provide state-of-the-art, affordable, easy-to-use, current worship resources to the student minister. Each volume includes audio CDs, both printed and PDF chord charts, Power Point files, and more. Because it *gathers songs from a broad range of publishers*, this resource would receive a high ranking. However, since the ongoing subscription is no longer available, its rating is somewhat moderated.

URL: http://www.spin360.com
Review: **SM35**

Telephone: (888) 697-7746
Mailing Address: SPIN
419 Dahlia Dr.
Brentwood, TN 37027

★★★☆☆

Mark Condon is a worship leader who has built an online club that releases songs on a monthly basis to the club members. There is a lot to like in this concept. He is joined by a cadre of well known songwriters and contributors, such as Israel Houghton, Ricardo Sanchez, Martha Munizzi and many others (of course, including Mark himself). You will normally get a selection of 3 songs each month. Each one comes with two MP3s (both full track and split track – very nice), PDF lead sheets, rhythm sheets and piano/vocal sheets (additional arrangement packages also get released depending on the song). The song selection is usually a collection of a popular released song (usually from the Integrity stable of music) and a couple songs from Mark or a friend (which will be new to most folks). You also get a monthly animated video background, or sometimes a video teaching. Overall, it is a nice package. If you want a good stream of songs for your praise and worship, it is worth a look.

URL: http://www.markcondoniclub.com
Review: **SM36**

Telephone: (614) 582-7537

Here we have listed resources for choral Periodical/Continuity clubs. Again, each of the entities listed offer an enrollment subscription program with varying content and costs. These typically offer new songs and/or arrangements that can be sent automatically to subscribers via download online or in a surface shipped package sent to a street address.

The Brentwood Choral Club and The Benson Choral Club are subscription services that allow users to preview new choral music as soon as it is released, so you always have the freshest, newest choral music available. Brentwood-Benson provides one of the largest and most popular choral preview services. Subscribers typically receive several different mailings per year, and each mailing can include resources such as a full-length listening CD, SATB choral songbook, DVD samplers, CD split tracks, and more. These items include arrangements by well known arrangers such as Russell Mauldin, J. Daniel Smith, Marty Hamby, Steven V. Taylor and others.

URL: http://www.brentwood-benson.com/choralclubs.aspx
Review: **SM37**

Telephone: (800) 546-2539
Mailing address: Brentwood-Benson
741 Cool Springs Blvd
Franklin, TN 37067

Lillenas Choral Club subscribers typically receive 4-6 different shipments per year, and each shipment includes full length audio preview CDs with written SATB scores of each new Lillenas published choral project. Often product rebate coupons and their newsletter are also included with subscription.

URL: http://bit.ly/dTKedU
Review: **SM38**

Telephone: (800) 363-2122
Mailing address: Lillenas Publishing Co.
Box 419527
Kansas City, MO 64141

Word Music Choral Club offers customized plans designed to meet your worship programming needs. Typically, each year users receive shipments that include complete printed and recorded demonstrations of every new choral release from Word Music and its labels. Each shipment will have from 3 to 6 new choral books for adults and children along with 11 to 15 (or more) new anthems for your adult choir, praise team or ensemble.

URL: http://www.wordmusic.com/choral-club
Review: **SM39**

Telephone: (888) 324-WORD (9673)
Mailing address: Word Music Choral Club
25 Music Square West
Nashville, TN 37203

Lifeway Worship Choral Club typically features new music throughout the year; each choral project has both a printed music songbook and full length audio CD. See details at their site.

URL: http://bit.ly/eIxiY1
Review: **SM40**

Telephone: (800) 436-3869
Mailing Addr: Lifeway Worship Choral Club
One Life Way Plaza MSN 160
Nashville, TN 37234-0160

Praise Gathering Choral Plan ships each May and November, with new releases from Randy Vader, Bill Rouse, Bill & Gloria Gaither, Camp Kirkland, Tom Fettke, Geron Davis, and others.

URL: http://bit.ly/gzxxAQ
Review: **SM41**

Telephone: (800) 436-3869
Mailing address: Praise Gathering Choral Plan
PO Box 350
Anderson, IN 46015

In a world where it seems that everything is going digital, you may ask — "Why talk about physical products?" The answer is multi-faceted, but important.

First, the majority of churches still purchase and use some physical products for audio, sheet music, and resources. Not everyone is online and not everyone likes to store their resource purchases on a computer disc that may vaporize, leaving them with all their purchases destroyed in an instant. Physical products provide a tactile resiliency and reality that is appreciated by many. Second, due to the ways in which music is sold and priced (due largely to the illegal and legal digitization of music) it is often now *more economical* to buy large collections of many songs on a physical resource. Publishers and labels have realized that they can put together 100 songs on a product and it simply saves the customer time compared to purchasing 100 different songs in a digital store. In the end, it is often cheaper to buy physical collections of 100 or more songs than to buy the equivalent songs one at a time in a digital download!

In this section are some examples of physical products for persons seeking to acquire new/additional worship songs. As noted above regarding the value of large collections, items listed here typically contain a lot of songs. We have chosen to omit "physical" resources with a small number of songs such as a typical album project songbook, instead focusing on compilation items larger in scope/content.

This is a very nice praise and worship collection created by well known worship leader Graham Kendrick. Lots of popular worship songs from the UK (as well as from North America and around the world) are included. *The Source* series currently *contains over 2,200 songs*. This series is dynamic and continues to grow, as they release more editions to *The Source*. It has keyboard friendly arrangements and exhaustive indexes. Also, these bound printed songbooks typically include a CD-ROM disk containing lyric word text files for every one of the 2,200+ songs. *The Source* books can be purchased through publisher Kevin Mayhew in the UK; and they can also be purchased in North America through "Brodt Music Company." Here are two respective online vendor web pages for *The Source* books.

>URL: http://bit.ly/ijTVIA (UK Buyers)
>URL: http://bit.ly/gRASW0 (US/North America)
>Review: **SM42**

Best of the Best (or commonly known as *BOB*) is a songbook from Fellowship Ministries including a nice selection of 253 popular favorite worship songs from all the major North American worship music publishers. *BOB* is best used by traditional churches moving to blended worship expressions or adding contemporary music for the first time, since its catalog of songs is made up of some of the earlier praise and worship music. It does not contain any songs from the last 10 years. Still, it is an excellent collection of songs pre-2000. Again, this resource is perfect for traditional churches that are adding contemporary style music.

It has an oversize "Accompaniment Edition" available, as a "Pew Edition," a "Lead Lines Edition," and also separately sold audio preview CDs, a lyrics presentation disk formatted for Power Point and SongShow Plus display software, and more. More details can be found at the publisher's web site.

URL: http://bit.ly/eVCW77
Review: **SM43**

The *More Songs for Praise & Worship* series songbooks are published by Word Music. After the original *Songs for Praise and Worship* songbook was released, there have subsequently been five additional numbered volumes also released in this songbook series with the titles: *More Songs for Praise & Worship* (*1*, *2*, *3*, *4* & *5*). Each of these contain a nice selection of contemporary-genre worship songs with the higher numbered editions containing the more recently released songs titles in chronological order. There is also a special volume in the series that's solely comprised of traditional hymns. Besides the standard Piano/Vocal/Guitar edition, each songbook in this series typically has several other editions available, such as separate editions for choir/worship team, keyboard, guitar, individual ensemble instruments and more. The original Songs for Praise and Worship songbook has gone into out-of-print status, but the five volumes of More Songs for Praise and Worship songbook are still available as of this writing.

URL: http://bit.ly/eRxkpU
Review: **SM44**

The *Celebration Hymnal* was created to offer a blended worship music songbook. Printed in 1997, it does not include any worship songs from the last 20 years. However, as a hymnal, it is *an excellent blend of classic worship songs and traditional hymns*. It has sold 2 million copies since its release.

URL: http://www.celebrationhymnal.com
Review: **SM45**

Vineyard Music Classics: Top 101 Worship Songs Of The Vineyard Songbook

Vineyard Top 101 is a bound songbook with paper pages that includes round note music notation for piano and vocals. It also includes a CD-ROM disk with printable PDF files of guitar charts in two keys, plus much more. This songbook can be purchased at the Vineyard Music web store at this URL:

URL: http://bit.ly/f5z3va
Review: **SM46**

The *Break Forth Worship Series* from Break Forth Ministries and Arlen Salte is an excellent blended worship collection. Besides the original *Break Forth Worship* songbook, there have also been at least 9 additional separate *Break Forth Update* supplement songbooks released to date. Separately sold, full song audio CDs are available corresponding to certain songs in the contents, and they have a "package" item for sale that includes the *Break Forth Worship* Songbook and Update #1-5 (210 songs in total). This series contains singable arrangements and a nice selection of contemporary-genre worship songs (there is an update that includes solely traditional hymns as well). More details can be found at the publisher's web site.

URL: http://bit.ly/hahydp
Review: **SM47**

The *Essential Modern Worship Fakebook* nice fake book format collection *includes 220 popular worship songs* in singable keys with a basic round note melody line notation written on a single treble staff, the written song lyrics printed below the staff, and guitar chord letter names written above the staff. This item also includes a bonus CD-ROM disk that has lots of enhanced content, including audio demonstration versions of all 220 songs, digital file enhanced chord charts, Nashville Number charts, lyric text files and overhead masters. This fake book can be purchased online from several vendors, including at the following Amazon.com web page.

URL: http://amzn.to/hzeQxL
Review: **SM48**

The *Worship Together Collection* series songs are compilations that each contain printed music notation for the songs from several individual Worship Together label album project audio recordings all included respectively within the contents of each one of the different songbooks. Each of these songbooks includes songs from 5-8 album project CDs all in one book (e.g. songs from worship album CDs by Matt Redman, Passion Band, Vicky Beeching, David Crowder, Chris Tomlin, Kutless, Third Day, Casting Crowns, Delirious?, etc). These songbooks can be purchased at several online music vendors. For example, we believe that both Encore Music and Stage Pass Music might have all of the nine volumes available at their web store URLs:

> http://www.encoremusic.com
> http://www.stagepass.com

When searching with an online search engine, the titles of these individual books are usually written this way: (i.e.) *Worship Together Songbook 2.0* and *Worship Together Songbook 8.0* and so on. The shortened Amazon link below is for the latest printed version (9.0), but you will find all versions are linked from this same page in Amazon (at the bottom of the page).

> URL: http://amzn.to/f3c4xm
> Review: **SM49**

The *Survivor Songbook* series has had at least 7 volume editions released to date, and their contemporary worship song selection is worth noting. Survivor Records is an imprint of Kingsway. These are hard to find anymore in North America, but I believe that the USA based River Of Life web store has several volumes available at http://www.riveroflifecbs.com . The entire series is available at Kingsway's UK based web store, but you can also find the first version (the most important in the series) at Amazon in the US at the following link.

URL: http://amzn.to/hlxJVV
Review: **SM50**

America's 200 Favorite Praise Choruses & Hymns Songbook published by Benson has a nice "blended" mix of traditional hymns, gospel songs, and older contemporary praise songs. While there are no songs included on it from the last 15 years, it has a treasure trove of material blended with classics before that. It is definitely worth reviewing. It can be purchased at several online music vendors, including Amazon.

URL: http://amzn.to/gKPkwm
Review: **SM51**

If you would like favorite songs from the Integrity/Hosanna catalog, the *Sing For Joy* songbook contains a collection of 100 time-tested Hosanna label songs. This particular volume has a good balance of upbeat praise songs and very melodic choruses of worship – truly taking a nice swath of great Hosanna songs. Because it was published in 2006, it is reasonably current, but contains plenty of Hosanna classics. It is very hard to find except through the publisher at this URL.

URL: http://bit.ly/ihco6s
Review: **SM52**

Of the several wedding compilations, the *Wedding & Love Fake Book* from Hal Leonard is worth noting. This "fake-book" format songbook contains the written lyrics, round note melody line notated on a single treble staff, and the guitar chords for each of the *500+ wedding songs*. Here is the Amazon location.

URL: http://amzn.to/icMzET
Review: **SM53**

Hal Leonard Songbooks

Hal Leonard has several Christian wedding songbooks, including *Songs for a Christian Wedding*, *Christian Wedding Songs*, *Contemporary Christian Wedding Songbook*, and *A Christian Wedding*. While they do not sell direct to the public, their site allows users to add items to a cart and the user is transferred to one of the independently operated web stores that carry the item.

URL: http://www.halleonard.com
Review: **SM54**

Finishing out our songs portion of this guide, this section contains examples of certain instructional resources for musicians. These are for persons and worship team members seeking to learn new/additional worship songs.

There are some excellent resources available with instructional information and lessons meant for teaching how to play a musical instrument (for example, how to tune and play an acoustic guitar, or how to play the piano). However, the items in this section are *not* that sort of thing. Instead, the items listed here are resources that presume some basic knowledge and familiarity with an instrument, and are meant to teach the user how to play specific songs from beginning to end. The items in this section each contain a collection of song titles in their respective contents, and for each song in the contents, they are meant to take the user through complete songs in a step by step method from beginning to end, walking the user through the songs demonstrating and teaching how to play the songs. Most of these allow users to *hear* how the songs are meant to sound, as they simultaneously *see* how to play the songs on their instrument. These items are somewhat new on the scene, and we have been asked about them with some on-going frequency, so we thought we would take a moment to mention and include a few important examples.

Vertical Music Worship Tools feature user-friendly arrangements of your favorite worship songs with instructional resources including a  printed songbook, instructional DVD, and an audio CD. Each DVD has on-screen graphics of charts or notes, along with split screen Guitar, Drum, Keyboard & Bass Cam Video. Several dozen individual volume items of these resources are available from Integrity/Vertical. The following URL leads you to the main page, where they can be located, reviewed and purchased.

URL: http://bit.ly/fDgIp1
Review: **SM55**

Vertical Music Worship Tools are also available online at WorshipTraining.com, but without the songbook and audio CD features (just the song teaching instructional videos). These tools are available to members of WorshipTraining.com only. The Vertical Tools are online at:

Bass Guitar: http://bit.ly/eMUFZM
Drums: http://bit.ly/eil3Gn
Piano/Keys: http://bit.ly/es6nMm
Acoustic Guitar: http://bit.ly/huFveO

Worship Band Play-Along resources are from Hal Leonard, and each individual item in the Worship Band Play-Along Series contains both an audio CD and a printed songbook bundled together into a single item. Bands can use the written music notation and chord charts to play "live" together in an ensemble, and individual band members can rehearse at home with the audio CD tracks. Worship leaders without a band can play/sing with the CD for a fuller sound. This series of resources allows users to learn to play the songs all the way through at their own pace. The included audio CD contains full performance demos and also separate accompaniment backing tracks. The CD is playable with any ordinary CD player, and it is also an "enhanced CD" for computer users so you can adjust the recording to any tempo without changing pitch. Each volume in the series offers five separate, correlated Book/CD packs for Guitar, Keyboard, Bass, Drum Set and Vocal. Drilling into the Hal Leonard website to find these can be tedious, so we have provided the best shortened link for this below.

URL: http://bit.ly/gCHcVk
Review: **SM56**

★★★★☆

Musicademy Song Learner Series DVDs are multimedia resources with a separate series for guitar,
keyboards, and bass guitar. These are excellent collection DVDs that help you learn the songs in the original style they are played, which is often important to using a song in a band or church setting.

URL: http://www.musicademy.com/store

Review: **SM57**

New Song Café

★★★☆☆

New Song Café Series DVDs feature songs by Passion and Worship Together songwriters. They are instructional and helpful video vignettes of the songs along with the techniques used by the writers and leaders on how to play them. This series is not sold in very many places, but they can be purchased at River Of Life online store.

URL: http://www.riveroflifecbs.com

Review: **SM58**

Vineyard Toolbox

Vineyard Toolbox DVDs have nice instructional content and work well for songs being used in both small group settings and large group settings. There are two toolbox DVD sets available – one for the *Sweetly Broken* album and one for the *Dwell* project. You can find them both here.

URL: http://bit.ly/fPvJ9x
Review: **SM59**

Keyboards – The Songs of Today

Keyboards – The Songs of Today is a good resource DVD from well known songwriter and clinician Ed Kerr. It features top 25 songs with Ed's insightful instruction on how to apply great technique to using and learning these songs for local churches. You can find the DVD at his web store at this address.

URL: http://bit.ly/fC7Jit
Review: **SM60**

On the Essential Worship Band, each volume is a 15 song DVD with on-screen instruction for your choice of Guitar, Bass, Keyboard or Drums that demonstrates chord-by-chord, measure-by-measure examples for every song. This resource includes custom solo-trax, chord charts, lead sheets and lyrics for each song.

> URL: http://bit.ly/fKjLWY
> Review: **SM61**

The Worship Team Director series is produced by Gateway Church. It is a complete training system with over 50 songs (in two volumes) for musicians. It also has vocal and visual presentation guide components that actually sync with the audio execution of the song. In addition to being a top notch training resource, this is an excellent 55 song modern worship collection.

> URL: http://amzn.to/gRCasg (Vol 1)
> URL: http://amzn.to/el9r9y (Vol 2)
> Review: **SM62**

Video and Image Media Sources

Video and media have become explosive new tools in the area of worship within the last 10 years. Finding good resources for video or images that can be used well in a local church can be difficult. This section helps with finding some top notch resources, both online and offline.

Online Media/Image Sites

Included here are some noted places along the Internet where one can acquire visual media resources for download online. Note that many places offer both downloadable items and also physical items on disk.

Worship House Media has been *the online creative trust for church video resources* for the last 2 years. Before that, the online world of media  was forming around this and two or three other top video resource sites. However, in the last couple of years, the quality of content, design of user interface, and organization of assets have lifted Worship House Media to the premier position as media provider for churches. Some top quality producers of media have stopped providing their content to multiple sites and focus on Worship House Media as their conduit to the church – and rightly so. Worship House Media, when taken as a complete solution, is clearly the preeminent site for worship media online. You won't have to wonder if the quality of media on this site will be professional or properly formatted for your computer. Worship House Media's quality control and meticulous care in providing excellent organization and search that churches can use make this site the safest and highest quality bet to find your top notch media quickly.

URL: http://www.worshiphousemedia.com

Review: **SM63**

The Work Of The People

The Work Of The People (TWOTP) is a producer of top notch worship media assets. Their work is particularly powerful and provocative. In the realm of media as a method of telling stories, there is none better than TWOTP. You won't find boring backgrounds or "hot and spicy" themes here, but you will find very real, human, authentic and sometimes provocative storytelling in film and image. Because of their focus, this site will not be the constant media filler that you could use every Sunday, week after week. But for specific projects and times when you want to say something with profound impact, if you have just one site to spend time on, this is one site you should check out.

What I love about TWOTP is their rooted focus on God and people. You won't be confused or drawn away by 3D outer space morphs or fractal graphs. TWOTP video stories are constantly contrasting the wonder and character of God with the reality of our humanity.

URL: http://www.theworkofthepeople.com
Review: **SM64**

★★★★☆

WorshipVue.com is a new online media
aggregator. Part of the PraiseCharts
family of online sites, WorshipVue has a glitzy user interface with
very good functionality. Two things stand out right away. First, the
search functionality is strong as it returns results quickly in nice
format for previewing and purchase. Second, the videos are clearly
categorized – mini movies, motion loops, countdowns and song
tracks. If you are a PraiseCharts fan, you will love WorshipVue,
because you can purchase media on WorshipVue using
PraiseCharts credits. Alternatively, you can purchase media directly
with a credit card (without using PraiseCharts credits). WorshipVue
is new, and this gives them the benefit of crafting a new site to the
needs of today's users. However, it also means that they start off
with a limited selection of content. Today, they have about 1000
videos online, a markedly smaller database than the main
competitors in this area. Videos are available in MPEG or
Quicktime formats. Be sure to check that the video you want is
available in the format you need. That said, the media content is
top notch, from some of the best producers in the fields. They are
definitely starting off on the right foot. Check them out!

URL: http://www.worshipvue.com
Review: **SM65**

Phone: (800) 921-4724
Mailing address: WorshipVue
Suite 123 #505-8840 210th Street
Langley, BC V1M 2Y2 / Canada

Where Worship House Media excels as the quality aggregator in this category, and The Work of The People emphasizes artistic and provocative of storytelling, Sermon Spice has become the Wal-Mart super store of online media. With more media than any other site, Sermon Spice contains a diverse and inexhaustible collection for churches. Part of the reason that Sermon Spice has so much more content than other site is that they encourage private individuals to submit media to Sermon Spices's commercial user library. They have an entire area for creative producers to become working video moguls. If you create a video that others might use in church, Sermon Spice might be the portal for you to get that video to the masses. The result? Sermon Spice has a surprisingly well defined mechanism for letting you see the top notch videos that people purchase and like. It exposes the best videos in each area, allowing you to glean the cream of the crop. That said, it also contains a significant portion of videos that are home-made and of less interest to discriminating media purchasers. The point is – with Sermon Spice, you may end up spending a bit more time searching for the top notch, perfect video, because it contains so much more content, and some of it is user generated. If you have the time, you might find a gem that fits your needs perfectly.

URL: http://sermonspice.com
Review: **SM66**

127

If you are looking to use the best selections of media from one of the top worship and arts ministries in the world, Willow Creek Arts has "Toward Wonder" videos. Quality will not be an issue on this site; everything is top notch. The selection and breadth of topic coverage is limited, as should be expected from a single producer. Still, their work is articulate, well-priced and like The Work of the People (another producer mentioned in this guide), is full of exceptional storytelling. All in all, it may be somewhat more palatable than The Work of the People for some churches as well. Toward Wonder/Pro Video has less of an artistic edge than The Work of the People, and is perhaps less gritty, but the site houses powerful and effective narratives in each video.

URL: http://www.towardwonder.com/prodvideo.asp

Review: **SM67**

When I am looking for a site that just does excellent color washes /images of background motions for lyrics/notes, there is one site that comes to mind. It is New Worship Media. While their quality is similar to what you might find on Worship House Media or Sermon Spice, they stay narrowly focused on just creating great color and spatial image backgrounds. These motion backgrounds use primarily gradients, washes, color mats, light bursts and fractal generations. I love this focus. If I want a quality motion background, do not need a sermon illustration, and just want to be sure I get a good selection and a quality product, New Worship Media is my first stop.

URL: http://newworshipmedia.com
Review: **SM68**

Bluefish TV

Bluefish TV has both downloadable and physical DVD items. This is a good site of collections of images and backgrounds. Its primary strength, however, is a collection of several media-centric curriculum options (from known speakers), and turnkey topical vignettes.

URL: http://www.bluefishtv.com

Review: **SM69**

Forty One Twenty / Church Media

Forty One Twenty is a site that has a consistent, strong artistic inventory of custom images and videos. You can tell the site is made by a single group or producer, since it has the same nuanced (and well done) approach to all the content. Some quality work is here, and you will not find any duds on this site. The site hosts a small collection of media that is artistic and well thought out – it is worth a look.

URL: http://www.fortyonetwenty.com
(note: once at the URL, drill down to "Church Media")

Review: **SM70**

★★★★☆

iStockphoto is one of the largest stock photo sites in the world for purchasing images. While it is not  a Christian specific site, it contains hundreds of thousands of quality images. I use this site as my first option for good quality, low cost stock photos for print and web pieces. If I want premium images beyond iStockphoto's content, I try Corbis. iStockphoto is not useful as a Christian search engine for background worship stuff – the Christian themed material is fairly average and without much edge. Stick to the Christian sites for Christian themed media. But for high quality stock photos, check here.

URL: http://www.istockphoto.com

Review: **SM71**

Corbis Images is perhaps the best professional image site online. Corbis is not a Christian site, but definitely a pro location for top quality images. Along with Getty Images, Corbis is considered one of the premier sources of top quality stock photo for professional marketing and image needs. You will pay more, but the quality of the image catalog is painstakingly culled to include only top notch media.

To be clear, Corbis is often used by producers themselves as source image and video for compositions. The same can be said of Getty Images and (to some degree) iStockphoto as well. These sites serve the professional designer and producer more than the niche church market, but in the purview of a seasoned media designer, this site can be a powerful asset.

URL: http://www.corbisimages.com
Review: **SM72**

Centerline New Media

Centerline New Media is a producer – making some of the best content appearing on other sites like Worship House Media. Their site warrants investigation. The site has a clean, crisp interface and nice options are available on each download. Notables: the site has theme packages such as their Easter package, and they have a collection of Spanish language media. Nice work, Centerline.

URL: http://centerlinenewmedia.com
Review: **SM73**

Beamer Films

Beamer Films is another producer whose acumen has made them one of the quality contributors to aggregators such as Worship House Media. What I love about Beamer is this – story telling. Each video is a focused illustration, meant to truly communicate something with visual power. They use imagery to make a compelling storyline come alive. Worth a look.

URL: http://www.beamerfilms.com
Review: **SM74**

There are a few sites that you can visit that have done everything perfectly. Dan Stevers is one of those. If you go to Dan's site you will find one of the premier producers of quality media for churches – anywhere in the world. Some of the pieces are CGI with a purpose and quality, others are motion stills. All of them contain perfect story, perfect images, perfect music, and perfect script. Go to his site and watch *God of the Broken*, *Voices of the Cross*, *Change the World*, and *We Give* or *Life With God*. Masterpiece works of media that are not over the top, but do not pull punches either, live here. Dan may be one of the best producers in the country, so he is not just pushing out a hundred new videos a year. There is a limited selection here, but every single piece is worth the money. Perfect. I do not hand out 5 stars for many resources, but Dan has earned it. Wow!

URL: http://www.danstevers.com
Review: **SM75**

What if you do not want a movie or a sermon illustration? What if all you want are motion backdrops for songs or looped motion backgrounds? One of the best places to find top quality song and service video backgrounds is Digital Stache. You won't find anything else really, but these are top quality, HD and SD motions. Pristine effects and attention to detail are found in each media piece. Unfortunately this site has a limited selection, but it does punctuate the focused and very well done work that is part of their SongKit and Looped sections. These are the two sections of the site that seem most relevant.

URL: http://digitalstache.com
Review: **SM76**

Video needs vary greatly across churches. But there are times when you have a need for triple-wide video. If you run a 3 screen system for your projection (and many moderate/large churches are now doing this), it can be tough to find good content for standard motion on songs or script presentation. Thr-ve answers the call and produces one of the only solid collections of triple-wide video motions on the market. If you need triple-wide, you better check out this site. Obviously this is an extremely niche site (and Thr-ve does produce other content for general worship media use) but their offering of triple-wide content is notably what makes them stand out. Thr-ve does not conform to the hope of ubiquitous format offerings, though, as they present just Quicktime MOV files, which is notably under expectations. But again, if you need triple-wide media, they are your huckleberry.

URL: http://www.thr-ve.com
Review: **SM77**

Pixelgirl Media

If you are looking for a place with bright, light-filled motions, look no further than Pixelgirl Media. Basically, every single motion background video is laminated with scintillating colors. Infusing spectral tracks, fractal morphs and reflective glares with various nuances, Pixelgirl delivers a collection that fills your need for anything bright, hopeful and glimmering that you might need. The site has nothing else, but again, what it does, it does well.

URL: http://pixelgirlmedia.com
Review: **SM78**

WorshipFilms.com

WorshipFilms.com features motion backgrounds, countdowns, sermon illustrations and even collections of hymns. This site contains an exceptional range of video file format/sizes, and is one of the longest running worship media sites. WorshipFilms is reasonably priced, and offers great package deal pricing. However, the site layout and navigation is a bit dated.

URL: http://www.worshipfilms.com
Review: **SM79**

A Visual Planet

A Visual Planet positions itself as real artists making real art for your ministry. It has some well-thought-out concepts and media. The collection is not as vast as other sites, but is still focused on Christian ministry. It has the feel of a mini Christian iStockphoto to this reviewer. This site has very good pricing, coupled with a more focused selection.

URL: http://www.avisualplanet.com

Review: **SM80**

Shift Worship

Shift Worship is worship media site with strong website navigation and a good image and video catalog. There is nothing amazing at this site. However, it is a quality resource you can use for your media backgrounds, stills and motions. Shift Worship focuses on countdowns and mini-movies for themed needs. This is not a site for stock photo needs other than lyric/text backgrounds.

URL: http://www.shiftworship.com

Review: **SM81**

Kinetic Faith

Kinetic Faith is a good site with content developed from a single local church. This site is free; however, it offers a very limited selection and a mediocre site layout. Kinetic Faith is intended as a free resource from one local church and not as a full service media site.

URL: http://www.kineticfaith.com
Review: **SM82**

Motion Worship

Motion Worship is a basic stock site with a few hundred videos online. Lyric backgrounds are this site's main focus, save a few count-down videos as well. It is reasonable quality stuff, and the more recent entries seem to be getting increasingly better in quality as the site adds content. This is a decent site with good navigation and reasonable site content. No edgy or breath-taking concepts here; just core content.

URL: http://www.motionworship.com
Review: **SM83**

Visual Worship

A more conservative take on visual images, this site has some good basic collections of content, but nothing very innovative. Everything is clear and pricing is reasonable. If you think that Worship House Media is too progressive for your church tastes, then this site might be a good option to keep things fairly predictable.

URL: http://www.visualworship.com

Review: **SM84**

Sharefaith

Sharefaith.com is a reasonable image catalog, good for bulletin content and design. It is a concise and conservative collection of motion and background images. More of a themed stock photo site for designing church printed materials than an on-screen media source, this site has a specific use in my opinion.

URL: http://www.sharefaith.com

Review: **SM85**

Sometimes it is required that you produce media on literally no budget. Below are some options. It will take you time to sift through the lousy images, but there is some gold in these sites for those who can take time to find it.

NOAA Photo Library (public domain) –
http://www.photolib.noaa.gov/index.html
Review: **SM86**

Bell's Christian Art Gallery –
http://www.jrbell.com/index.html
Review: **SM87**

Church Media Exchange Center –
http://www.churchmedia.net/MXC
Review: **SM88**

FreeFoto.com –
http://www.freefoto.com/index.jsp
Review: **SM89**

Physical Media/Image Sources

The following are places that sell physical DVD/image products on disc. They may also sell online via download as well, but they are mostly producers whose media also appears on other sites. We felt these sites these were worth mentioning uniquely, since some churches prefer to buy physical, packaged image and video resources.

Midnight Oil

Midnight Oil has been around a while and has a good reputation for quality, useful videos. Midnight Oil is one of the few places that have been around for a long time producing illustration and video media. They are digital storytellers, and have kept the church in mind by continuing to provide DVDs for churches that would rather use physical product.

URL: http://www.midnightoilproductions.com
Review: **SM90**

Highway Media

Highway Media is the oldest member of the online media sources for churches. Literally two decades of doing video media has given this company a reputation to match. A strong producer with a newly re-launched website, Highway Media is a good one to check out. Highway Media (formerly Highway Video) is considered the "elder statesmen" of video producers and were the first ones to bring video storytelling to churches in a big way. They are still producing excellent original video and media.

URL: http://www.highwaymedia.org
Review: **SM91**

Nooma Films

Nooma Films is a creative trust that contains the storytelling/teaching videos from Rob Bell and Francis Chan. Perhaps the best narrative framed videos on the market, the production values are stellar and delivery is perfect. No other content here, but if you are looking for vignettes with brilliant delivery and you like the conclusions these speakers bring to the table, you will be in love with this site. They get 12 out of 10 for quality. It is definitely worth your time to visit this site at least to see a few preview videos. (DVD & Download available)

URL: http://store.flannel.org/films.html
Review: **SM92**

Digital HotCakes

Digital HotCakes is a reasonable collection of digital media, at a reasonable price. Nothing surprising here, but a good, reasonable site for various media needs.

URL: http://www.digitalhotcakes.com
Review: **SM93**

ImageVine

ImageVine is a collection of digital media, at a very reasonable price. A reasonable site for basic motions and worship lyric background needs.

      URL: http://www.imagevine.com
      Review: **SM94**

Good Salt

According to their website they are the "world's leading source of religious imagery." That might be true of the quantity and intent, but the quality varies greatly across the images on this site. Still, here are a vast number of applications for the images here. Good Salt is better described as an image site for paintings, drawings and themed stock photo (some generated images as well) for ministry uses, not just Sunday morning.

      URL: http://www.goodsalt.com
      Review: **SM95**

Song-Based Media/Image Products

Song based accompaniment DVD resources are a special kind of DVD with on-screen written lyrics display and corresponding audio accompaniment music that are specifically intended for use in congregational worship singing settings. The idea is that users play back the DVD (or video media file), and the congregation sings along with their own voices by reading the written song lyrics on the view-screen as they hear the directly corresponding audio accompaniment music emanating from the sound system speakers. Depending on the resource, the video and lyrics can accompany a recorded audio track (embedded in the video) or can be played in synchronization with a live person/group that is performing the music.

This is a new era of "plug and play" media that was launched largely by the iWorship DVD series from Integrity Media, which has become the gold standard in this resource type.

Worship Backing Band For Churches and Small Groups from Musicademy includes 54 songs,  and there is an edition for use in congregational singing settings, and another edition designed as practice tracks for worship band members. Excellent resource. Here is the official web site.

URL: http://bit.ly/ekAhQM
Review: **SM96**

iWorship series DVDs from Integrity music come in single-song disks and also in multi-song disks. There are several different formats of iWorship DVD video; some of the iWorship "accompaniment DVD" items are designed to be played back exclusively in a stand-alone component DVD player, like the ordinary kind of component DVD player one might find connected by cables to a TV in a home living room. Available on their official web store.

URL: http://bit.ly/h6DHEV
Review: **SM97**

iWorship MPEG Video Library

In contrast to iWorship DVDs, the iWorship MPEG Video Library DVD-ROM items are meant for users who want to copy the song files onto a computer hard drive and then use a computer display software program and digital projection system to display the songs to the congregation/audience. Again this is available on their official web store.

URL: http://bit.ly/hHeaxL
Review: **SM98**

iWorship Flexx

iWorship Flexx is the most powerful of the song-based video resources. These MPEG and H.264 format videos are broken up so that each song segment is on a separate file. This allows tech-savvy users to map a song during performance, with video, lyrics and audio (if desired) truly following the worship leader. Requires software such as MediaShout or ProPresenter.

URL: http://bit.ly/fNKedm
Review: **SM99**

Word Music Visual Trax DVDs are single-song accompaniment DVDs. In addition to the visual tracks, they have regular performance tracks as well at the publisher's web page.

URL: http://bit.ly/erJTye
Review: **SM100**

Worship Together Visual – Here I Am To Worship DVD has dual formats on the disk so it will playback in a stand-alone component DVD player. The songs can also be copied onto a computer hard drive and then used with a computer display software program and digital projection system. You can purchase it online at this URL:

URL: http://bit.ly/eiDAwh
Review: **SM101**

Appendix: Ultimate Worship Resource Guide – Online Tools

With your purchase of this book, you and your church also have one year of membership access to the official website of the UltimateWorshipResourceGuide.com. This allows you and your church to access the web links mentioned in this book, including any updated information that may be pertinent to the resource you are interested in. This book took many hours to complete, and your purchase of this book makes that work possible. You are welcome to give your access to the website out to anyone else in your church, but please do not give it out beyond that. We rely on your honesty to make publishing this guide a possibility.

To login:

1. Go to www.UltimateWorshipResourceGuide.com
2. Click "Member Login"
3. Enter the 10-digit ISBN for this book as your access code. You can find the 10-digit ISBN on Page 6.

Acknowledgements

Any writing is a collective effort, not only of the presented text, but of the hours, days and years of knowledge and experience the text represents. That is doubly true when creating a guide of this type. In the last 15 years, I have learned more from others than I could possibly give acknowledgement to here. The years spent working at WorshipMusic.com changed my life from being interested in resourcing the church to being committed to it. This book is a direct outgrowth of that time and the ministry we found in serving the Body of Christ. Along the way, I had the chance to work with many wonderful people who have stood out and deeply impacted both my life and this volume.

Foremost of those impacting this book is Martin Caffrey, who was my research assistant for this project. Aside from his work here, he worked with us for many years at WorshipMusic.com, where his knowledge and expertise impacted literally thousands of customers and churches across the world. Thanks also to Matt Frise, who contributed to interior diagram design and photography.

I am very thankful for the encouragement and support of my brother, Lockley Gentes, who was the iron will and mind of clarity behind so much of the resourcing work we did for over 10 years at WorshipMusic.com. I am grateful for Marc Dooley, Andy Molenda, Reggie Magana, David Wright, Joshua Walsh, Jordan Gentes and especially Lori Lindsey and Jeremy Dunn for their years of partnership in offering their service to resource the global church.

While being involved in worship resourcing we were inexorably connected to the Christian music industry. Those years allowed me to learn from, and partner with, a number of leaders who have deeply impacted my work and, hence, this volume. Primary of those is Dan Wilt who not only served as editor for this volume but is a leader, visionary and friend who has changed many lives irrevocably, through his call to teach the nations to worship. I have been one of those. Others, who have been great partners and encouragers in the business of music and ministry are Arlen Salte, Chris Long, Craig Dunnagan, Mark Powell, Kevin Weimer, Jerry Weimer, Don Moen, Dave Williamson, Marc Pusch, Casey Corum and Jason Hagen.

Thanks also to my three sons, who not only supported me through the uncountable hours of working at home to complete this project, but who have also taught me the wonder of worship through their own personal pursuits of God.

Thanks most especially to my friend, lover and wife, Carol. There are no words to communicate my thanks for your love and support.

Thanks to God. My father, my friend – you set about to equip your church through the Holy Spirit – thank you for allowing me to join in.

Kim Gentes is at the center of many of today's most pivotal conversations about worship, and the music we use in worship. As a worship leader, songwriter, recording artist and freelance writer, Kim has been a featured speaker and  worship leader at events across the US and Canada.

With his core passion to equip worship leaders and teams in the work of creative ministry, Kim founded WorshipMusic.com in 1998, with his brother Lockley, and grew it into the largest independent online supplier of worship resources in the world. Through that, and other initiatives, he has been at the forefront of resourcing the global church in worship for over 15 years – reaching tens of thousands of churches worldwide. Kim has written for popular magazines such as *Worship Leader Magazine*, *Inside Worship Magazine* and others.

In addition to equipping the international church in worship through his work and ministry, he has been a local worship leader in Vineyard churches in the Phoenix, Arizona metro area and more recently in the Nashville area. Originally from Canada, Kim and his wife Carol spent 20 years in Arizona before moving to Franklin, TN, where they now live with their 3 boys.

Author photo courtesy of Matt Frise (www.mattfrise.com).

A Visual Planet, 138
acoustic guitar, 41
America's 200 Favorite Praise Choruses & Hymns Songbook, 114
Arlen Salte, 19, 110
Beamer Films, 133
Bell's Christian Art Gallery, 141
Best of the Best In Contemporary Praise & Worship, 107
Billy Funk, 35
Bluefish TV, 130
Bob Fitts, 35
Break Forth, 110
Brentwood-Benson, 77, 87, 100, 114
Calvary Chapel, 34, 35
CCLI, 67, 82
CD-ROM, 44, 88, 89, 109, 111
Celebration Hymnal, 109
Centerline New Media, 133
Charlie Hall, 37
children's worship, 35
choral, 35, 99, 100, 101, 102, 103, 104
chord chart, 42
Chris Tomlin, 37, 49
Christian radio, 49, 50
Christian Virtual Hymnal, 90
Church Media Exchange Center, 141
Club Vineyard, 95
Contemporary Christian Music, 34
continuity clubs, 44
Corbis Images, 61, 132
Cyber Hymnal, 81
Dan Stevers, 61, 134
Daniel Gardner, 35

Darlene Zschech, 36
David and Dale Garratt, 34
David Crowder, 37
Delirious?, 36
Digital HotCakes, 145
Digital Sheet Music Library, 88
Digital Stache, 135
Digital Worship News, 68
DiscoverWorship.com, 76
Don Moen, 35
DVD, 86, 88, 100, 118, 120, 121, 122, 130, 143, 145, 147, 148, 150
DVD-ROM, 86, 149
Ed Kerr, 121
EMI, 36, 64, 66, 86, 89, 111, 112, 120
Essential Worship Band, 122
fake book, 87, 111
Fellowship Ministries, 107
Forty One Twenty, 130
FreeFoto.com, 141
garage band musicians, 42
Gary Sadler, 35
Good Salt, 146
gospel, 35
Graham Kendrick, 34, 106
GreatWorshipSongs.com, 77
H.264, 149
Hal Leonard, 116, 119
Highway Media, 144
Hillsong Australia, 36, 38
Hosanna Music, 35
Hungry, 37
hymnal, 45, 47
Hymnal.net, 81
HymnCharts.com, 61, 74
hymns, 43, 74, 81, 90, 109
ImageVine, 146

Integrity Music, 35, 65, 66, 72, 88, 89, 115, 118, 122
Integrity's Hosanna, 44
IntegritySongs.com, 65
ION Worship, 79
Israel Houghton, 38
iStockphoto, 131
iWorship, 61, 88, 148, 149
iWorship Flexx, 61, 149
iWorship MPEG Video Library, 61, 149
J.W. Pepper, 80
Jesus Culture music, 50
Jesus People, 34
Kent Henry, 35
Keyboards – The Songs of Today, 121
Kim Gentes, 69, 157
Kinetic Faith, 139
Kingsway Music, 36, 37, 48, 79, 113
Lenny LeBlanc, 35
Lifeway, 75, 103
LifewayWorship.com, 75
Lillenas, 101
Lynn Deshazo, 35
Maranatha Green Book, 44
Maranatha Music, 34, 35
Maranatha Praise, 44
Maranatha Red Book, 44
Mark Condon, 97
Marty Nystrom, 35
Matt Redman, 36, 38
melodic songwriting, 41
membership access, 153
Michael W. Smith, 37, 38, 49
Midnight Oil, 144
More Songs for Praise & Worship, 44, 108
Motion Worship, 139
MPEG, 61, 126, 149
Musicademy, 120, 148

Musicademy Song Learner Series, 120
musicals, 35
MusicNotes.com, 83, 84
New Song Café, 120
New Worship Media, 129
NOAA Photo Library, 141
Nooma Films, 61, 145
overhead transparencies, 43
Passion movement, 37
Paul Baloche, 38, 89
Pixelgirl Media, 137
Praise Gathering, 104
PraiseCharts.com, 61, 73, 126
presentation system, 43
Quicktime, 126
R&B, 35
reviews, 69
Revivial Generation, 48
Ron Kenoly, 35
SATB, 41
Sermon Spice, 127
Sharefaith.com, 140
SheetMusicPlus.com, 83
Shift Worship, 138
Sing For Joy, 115
sixsteps Records, 37
SOFTPraise, 91
songbook, 106, 107, 108, 109, 110, 113, 114, 115, 116, 118, 119
SongDiscovery, 69, 94
SongQuery.com, 68
Songs of the Vineyard, 44
SongSelect, 82
Sonicflood, 37, 49
Soul Survivor, 36, 37
Spin360, 96
Survivor Songbook, 113
technology, 43, 45
The Praise and Worship Song Book, 61, 87

The Source, 106
The Work Of The People, 125
Third Day, 49
Thr-ve, 136
Tim Hughes, 36, 38
Tom Brooks, 35
Touching the Father's Heart, 44
Toward Wonder, 128
Vertical Music Worship Tools, 118
Vineyard Music, 35, 36, 66, 72, 78, 79, 95, 109, 121
VisualWorship.com, 140
wedding songs, 116
Willow Creek Arts, 128
Word, 66, 72, 77, 102, 108, 150
WordMusicNow.com, 77

Worship Backing Band, 148
Worship Band Play-Along, 119
Worship Team Director, 122
worship wars, 39
WorshipFilms.com, 137
WorshipHouseMedia.com, 61, 124
WorshipMusic.com, 37
WorshipTeam.com, 61, 66, 72
WorshipTogether.com, 48, 64, 66, 86, 89, 112, 120, 150
WorshipVue.com, 126
X.0: The Digital Hymnal for the Modern Worship Generation, 61, 86
YouTube, 44

161

Made in the USA
Charleston, SC
20 May 2011